Life Cycles

Everything from
start to finish

Penguin Random House

Authors and consultants:
Lead consultant Derek Harvey
Plants and animals authors Steve Setford, Lucy Spelman, Emily Keeble, Klint Janulis, Richard Walker
Space author and consultant Sophie Allan
Earth author and consultant Anthea Lacchia
Illustrated by Sam Falconer

Senior editor Marie Greenwood
Senior commissioning designer Joanne Clark
Editors Abby Aitcheson, Jolyon Goddard
Editorial assistant Seeta Parmar
Designers Katie Knutton, Robert Perry
US Editor Elizabeth Searcy
US Senior editor Shannon Beatty
DTP designer Vijay Kandwal
Picture researcher Sakshi Saluja

Managing editor Jonathan Melmoth
Managing art editor Diane Peyton Jones
Pre-Producer Dragana Puvacic
Producer Inderjit Bhullar
Publishing director Sarah Larter

First American Edition, 2020
Published in the United States by DK Publishing
1745 Broadway, 20th Floor, New York, NY 10019

Published in Great Britain by Dorling Kindersley Limited.

A catalog record for this book is available from
the Library of Congress.
ISBN: 978-1-4654-9744-4

DK books are available at special discounts when purchased in bulk for sales promotions, premiums, fund-raising, or educational use. For details, contact: DK Publishing Special Markets,
1745 Broadway, 20th Floor, New York, NY 10019
SpecialSales@dk.com

Printed and bound in China

All images © Dorling Kindersley Limited

www.dk.com

Life Cycles

Everything from start to finish

Contents

Animals

Animals are arranged in the following order: invertebrates, fish, amphibians, reptiles, birds, and mammals.

What is a *life cycle?*

Birds, and most reptiles and amphibians, lay fertilized eggs that develop outside the mother's body.

Life is always changing, but it follows patterns too. Living things—including ourselves—grow, produce young, and die. There are repeating processes for nonliving things too, from mountains, rocks, and rivers to planets, comets, and stars. We call all these patterns life cycles.

Life cycles are interlinked. Plants take nutrients and water from the soil and energy from sunlight. Animals eat plants or other animals in order to grow. Many plants rely on animals such as insects to spread their pollen so they can make seeds and reproduce. When plants and animals die, their remains rot and become part of the soil that will nourish new plants.

The life cycles we see around us appear endless. Birth and growth are balanced by breakdown and decay. Yet these cycles can be fragile. Change—whether natural or caused by humans—can disrupt them. Vulnerable species may dwindle to extinction when their cycles get broken, while—over millions of years— new species emerge by evolution.

Earth and space

Our Earth is constantly changing. Rocks wear away and get recycled into new rocks, while water circulates between sea, sky, and land. In space, comets and stars form from gas and dust, burn out, then return to gas and dust.

Earth's life cycles are tiny fractions of the age of the universe: 13.8 billion years.

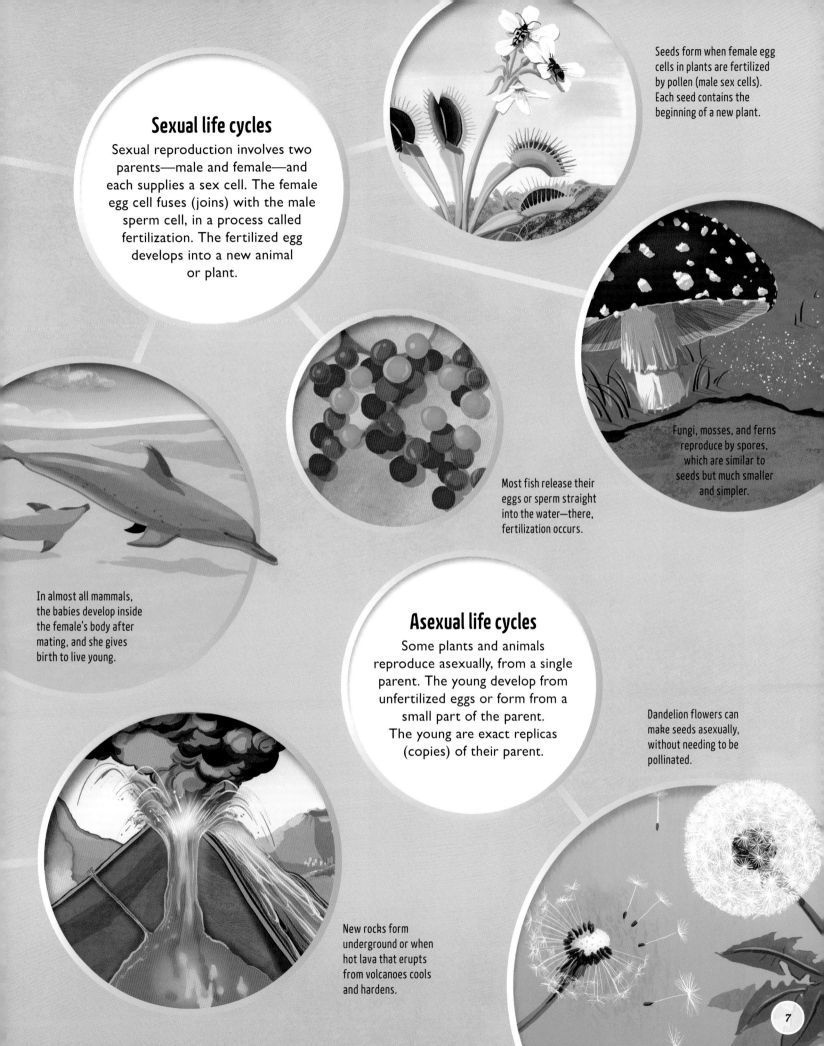

Sexual life cycles

Sexual reproduction involves two parents—male and female—and each supplies a sex cell. The female egg cell fuses (joins) with the male sperm cell, in a process called fertilization. The fertilized egg develops into a new animal or plant.

Seeds form when female egg cells in plants are fertilized by pollen (male sex cells). Each seed contains the beginning of a new plant.

Fungi, mosses, and ferns reproduce by spores, which are similar to seeds but much smaller and simpler.

Most fish release their eggs or sperm straight into the water—there, fertilization occurs.

In almost all mammals, the babies develop inside the female's body after mating, and she gives birth to live young.

Asexual life cycles

Some plants and animals reproduce asexually, from a single parent. The young develop from unfertilized eggs or form from a small part of the parent. The young are exact replicas (copies) of their parent.

Dandelion flowers can make seeds asexually, without needing to be pollinated.

New rocks form underground or when hot lava that erupts from volcanoes cools and hardens.

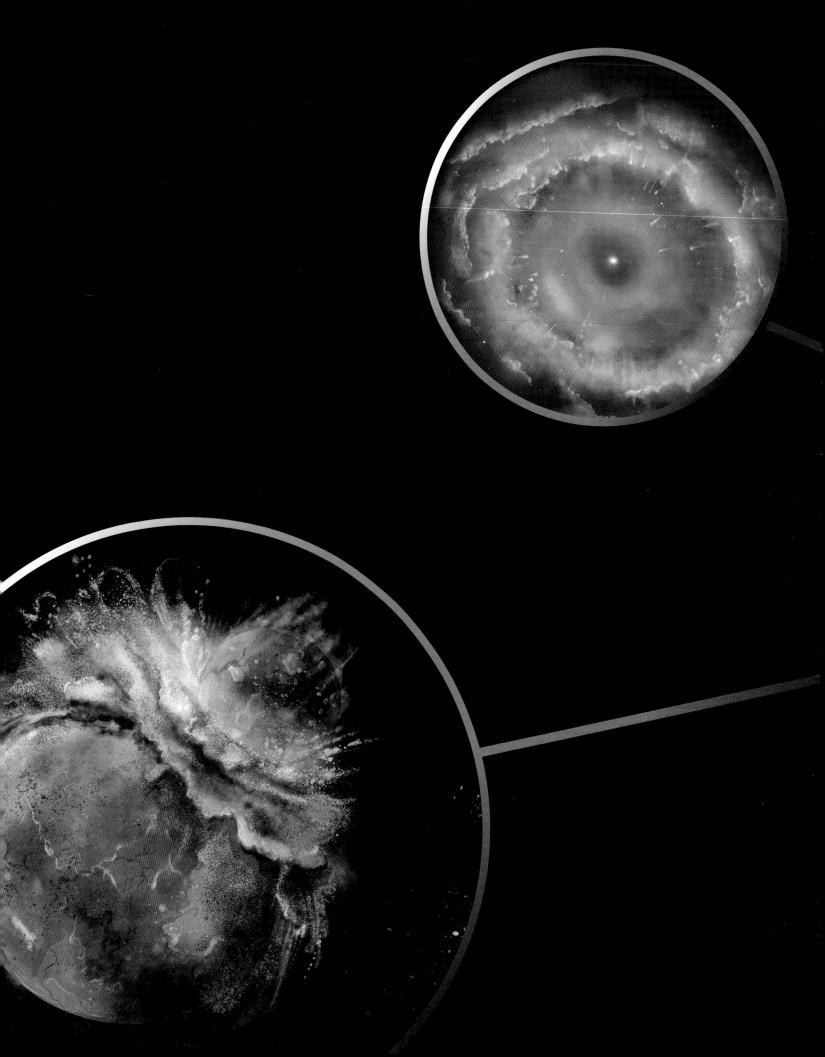

Space

Space is unimaginably huge and full of exciting things, such as planets, moons, galaxies, and black holes. It is also constantly changing—stars form from beautiful clouds of dust and gas, evolve through their life cycle to slowly die away, or go out with an enormous bang. Everything that has or will ever be formed was created in space—including the building blocks of you!

After less than a second, quarks formed.

The big bang

More than 13 billion years ago, the universe began as a tiny point, smaller than a grain of salt. In a single huge explosion, the universe, including space and time, sprang into existence. As it expanded in all directions, it began to cool down.

At this point, the temperature of the universe was more than 1.8 billion °F (1 billion °C).

This early light of the universe still exists as a faint glow of radiation.

A few minutes old

Quarks—the building blocks of all materials—formed tiny subatomic particles called protons and neutrons. The universe was now cool enough to let these particles combine to become simple nuclei— the centers of atoms.

380,000 years old

The universe was finally cool enough for the nuclei to grab hold of electrons, forming complete atoms. The universe became an expanding, swirling mass of gas.

300 million years old

Over time, the gas of the universe was pulled into clumps by gravity. As these clumps collapsed, they got hot and the first stars were born.

See also
Find out how stars form (12–13) and how the solar system (14–15) and the moon (16–17) were made.

The universe

Our universe is everything there is—galaxies, stars, planets, moons, and even space and time. The universe is so incredible and vast that it is difficult to fully understand it. We on planet Earth are just one tiny speck in the universe, and it will perhaps always remain a mystery to us.

Georges Lemaître In 1927, Belgian astronomer Georges Lemaître was the first person to suggest the universe started with a big bang. At the time, few astronomers believed him.

The Hubble Space Telescope This special telescope has taken hundreds of pictures of space. Inside one tiny, dark patch, astronomers found 10,000 distant galaxies, each containing hundreds of billions of stars.

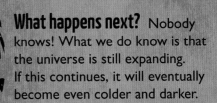

Early stars were massive and produced heavy elements that would one day form planets.

Our galaxy, the Milky Way, is one of the oldest in the universe.

What happens next? Nobody knows! What we do know is that the universe is still expanding. If this continues, it will eventually become even colder and darker.

Galaxies are pushed apart as the universe expands.

500 million years old

These stars were pulled together by gravity into collections of hundreds of billions of stars to form the first galaxies, including our own Milky Way.

13.8 billion years old

Today, the universe is still expanding. It is a vast collection of galaxies, gas, and strange things we are still trying to understand.

Birth

Each stage of a star's life cycle takes place over billions of years. All stars are born from giant gas and dust clouds, called nebulae. Gravity pulls the gas and dust together to form hot, spinning clumps.

Young and bright

Over time, these clumps get so hot that nuclear reactions start inside them, and they turn into stars. The intense heat makes them glow. A young star is called a protostar—*proto* means *early*.

Death

The planetary nebula drifts away and is scattered into space, where it will in time form new stars. All that is left of the star is the glowing core, called a white dwarf. This gets smaller until it cools and becomes a black dwarf.

Star

Just like animals, stars are born, grow and develop through life, and then die. Depending on its type and size, a star can live and die in different ways. Bigger stars shine more brightly but live shorter lives than smaller stars. This is the life cycle of a medium-sized star.

The sun The sun is a medium-sized star and will follow the same life cycle as the one above. The sun formed about 4.6 billion years ago and is presently at the main-sequence stage. In about 5 billion years, it will die.

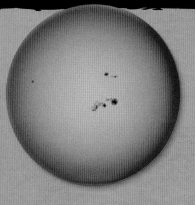

Black dwarf Stars die in different ways. Medium-sized stars become dark, dead blobs called black dwarfs. Bigger stars collapse into themselves completely. They turn into black holes. Here, gravity is so strong that no light can escape.

Middle years

Gradually, the star gets even hotter and shines brighter. As it heats up, the gases, including hydrogen, ignite and start to burn up. The star spends most of its life at this stage, called the main-sequence stage.

Getting bigger

After billions of years, the star runs out of hydrogen in its core. The star expands to a huge size, and the temperature of its outer shell drops, causing the star to glow red. It is now called a red giant.

Fading and dying

Once all the fuel is used up, the outer layers of the red giant start to fall away. This glowing cloud of material is called a planetary nebula.

See also
Find out how the universe formed (10–11) and how the planets and the sun came into being (14–15).

Heating up A star's color depends on how hot it is. The hottest stars produce a blue light. Cooler stars have a reddish-orangy light. It is possible to see these differently colored stars if you look at the sky through binoculars on a clear night.

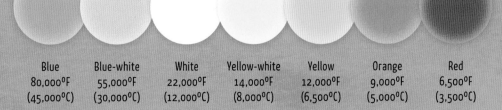

Blue	Blue-white	White	Yellow-white	Yellow	Orange	Red
80,000°F	55,000°F	22,000°F	14,000°F	12,000°F	9,000°F	6,500°F
(45,000°C)	(30,000°C)	(12,000°C)	(8,000°C)	(6,500°C)	(5,000°C)	(3,500°C)

The sun is born

As the cloud collapsed due to gravity, its center started to heat up. It eventually became so hot that hydrogen atoms combined to make helium, in a process called fusion. This released a huge amount of energy, and a hot, shining star was born—the sun.

Some of the lightest gases spun out to the cold outer edge of the disk.

Planets forming

Material from the cloud began to form planets. Close to the sun, gravity pulled bits of dust together into clumps to form rocky planets. Farther away, where it was cooler, gases came together to form enormous planets called gas giants.

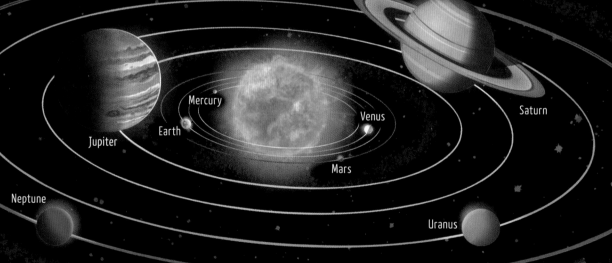

Mercury

Venus

Earth

Jupiter

Mars

Saturn

Neptune

Uranus

See also
Find out more about our universe (10–11) and how stars form (12–13).

Our solar system

It took tens of millions of years for the planets to form our solar system. Mercury, Venus, Earth, and Mars are rocky planets, and Jupiter, Saturn, Uranus, and Neptune are gas giants. Between Mars and Jupiter is an area called the asteroid belt. This contains many smaller dwarf planets, as well as small rocky asteroids.

Beyond Neptune's orbit, the frozen gases formed comets.

Dusty beginnings

About 4.6 billion years ago, a cloud of dust and gas began to fall in on itself. As it collapsed, it started to spin, forming a dense disk shape.

This is the area of our solar system where water and life can exist. Like the porridge that Goldilocks eats, the conditions are perfect—it's neither too far from nor too close to the sun.

The solar system

The solar system is our home. A neighborhood of planets, moons, asteroids, and comets that dance in a cosmic ring around our star, the sun. And while the sun keeps everything going around it, locked in its gravity, it also holds the key to our solar system's future.

When the sun expands, this zone will move away from Earth. Eventually, some of the gas giants and their moons will be in the Goldilocks zone.

What next?

At the moment, our solar system is pretty stable. However, in about five billion years' time, the sun will run out of hydrogen and begin to burn helium. When this happens, it will swell up and cool down until it turns into a red giant—a type of star entering a late stage of its life—gobbling up Mercury, Venus, and maybe even the Earth!

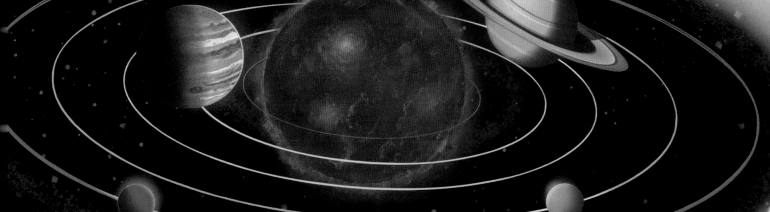

Collision in space

The collision with Earth destroyed Theia. Huge amounts of material from both planets were thrown into space. Melted rock from Theia combined with the Earth.

Forming the moon

The material from this collision was spun out into orbit around the Earth. Then it began to be pulled together by gravity to form the moon—a hot ball of melted rock a quarter of the size of the Earth.

The moon

Now our constant companion in space, the moon is thought to have been created 4.5 billion years ago. When the Earth was still very young, it was a hot, melted ball of rock and metal. A small Mars-sized planet called Theia collided with Earth, and the moon was born.

See also
Find out more about the solar system (14–15) and comets (18–19).

Lunar seas The side of the moon that faces us is covered in dark areas, or "seas"—so called because early astronomers thought they were real seas! They were formed about a billion years ago when melted rock, called magma, rose up to the surface and cooled.

Eclipse Sometimes, the sun, moon, and Earth are perfectly aligned so that as the moon passes between the sun and Earth, it is just the right size to perfectly cover (eclipse) the sun.

Asteroids and comets

As the moon cooled, a crust of solid rock formed on its surface. For the next 500 million years, the moon and Earth were pounded by small objects made of rock and ice, called asteroids and comets.

The moon is moving away from Earth at a rate of 1.5 in (4 cm) per year.

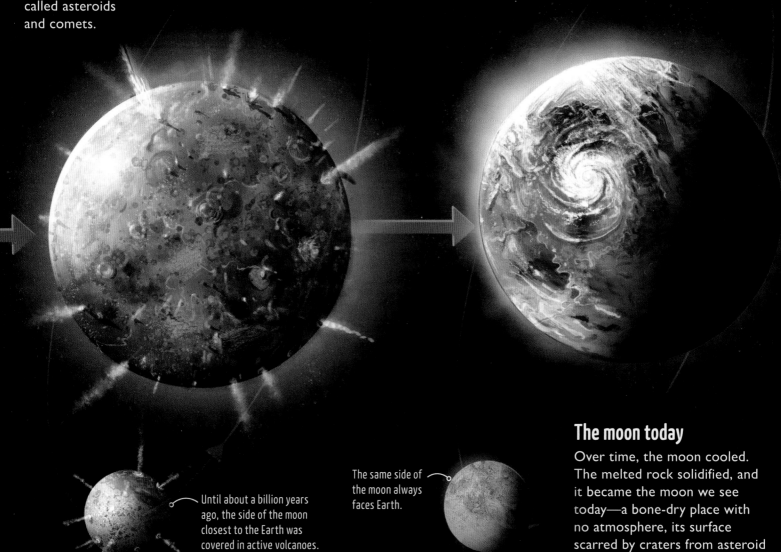

Until about a billion years ago, the side of the moon closest to the Earth was covered in active volcanoes.

The same side of the moon always faces Earth.

The moon today

Over time, the moon cooled. The melted rock solidified, and it became the moon we see today—a bone-dry place with no atmosphere, its surface scarred by craters from asteroid impacts. The moon now orbits the Earth, going around it once every 27.3 days.

Tides The moon affects the ocean tides. Gravity pulls at the water on Earth, causing it to bulge out. As the moon orbits the Earth, it pulls this water bulge with it, which makes sea levels rise and fall. These movements are the tides.

17

Impact crater

Impact crater Though it is rare, comets and meteorites can slam into the Earth with huge amounts of force. This leaves large impact craters, such as this one in Arizona. We even think a comet impact wiped out the dinosaurs!

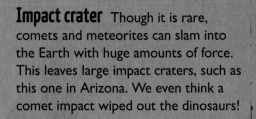

Two tails A comet actually has two tails—a dust tail that stretches out behind it, and a gas tail that is pushed away from the sun by solar winds.

Rosetta The European space probe *Rosetta* reached Comet 67P in 2014. The probe released a lander called *Philae*, which was the first object to ever land on a comet and helped scientists learn a lot more about them.

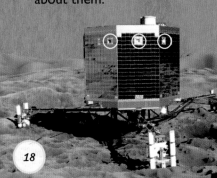

Comet

Comets are frozen, dusty worlds created from material that was left over after our solar system formed. Some comets are so far away from the sun that we can't see them even with telescopes. However, many others have been spotted in the night sky.

Comets spend most of their time in an area called the Kuiper Belt at the edge of our solar system.

A comet can be pushed out of the Kuiper Belt after colliding with another comet.

Rocky beginnings

Far away from the sun, it is so cold that water and gases freeze, collecting on the surface of dust. These materials start to be pulled together by gravity, forming icy rocks that continue to combine until eventually, a huge icy, rocky comet is formed.

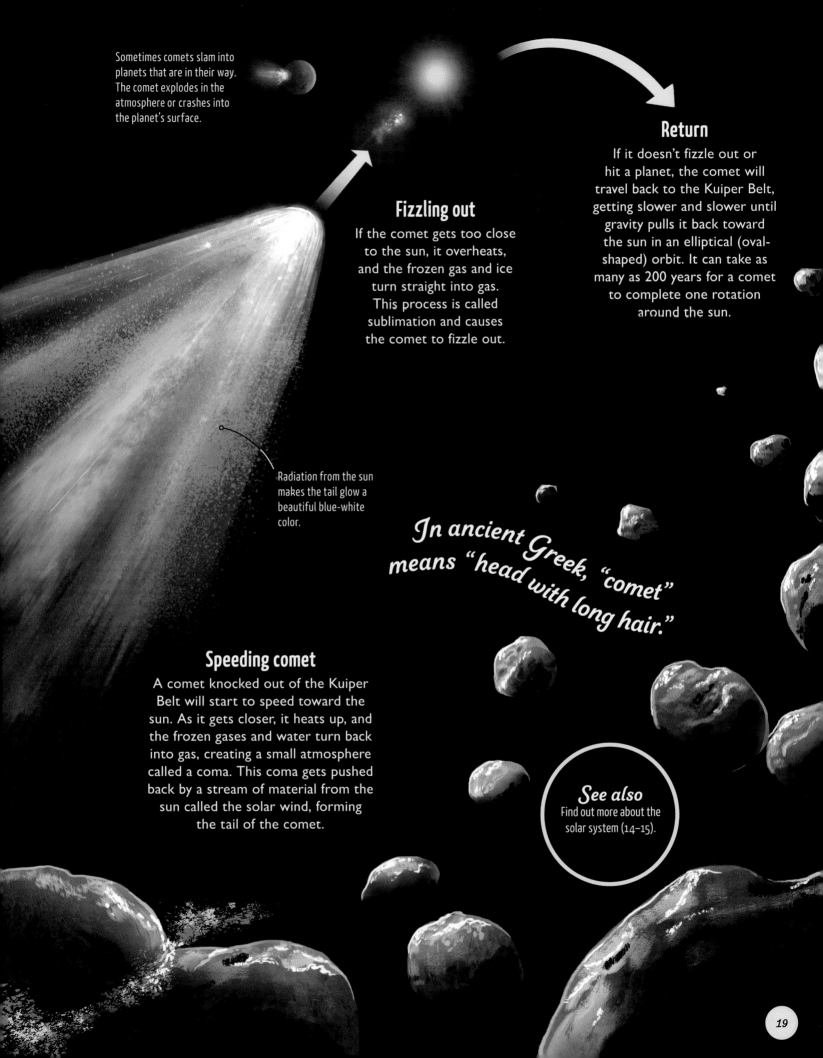

Sometimes comets slam into planets that are in their way. The comet explodes in the atmosphere or crashes into the planet's surface.

Return

If it doesn't fizzle out or hit a planet, the comet will travel back to the Kuiper Belt, getting slower and slower until gravity pulls it back toward the sun in an elliptical (oval-shaped) orbit. It can take as many as 200 years for a comet to complete one rotation around the sun.

Fizzling out

If the comet gets too close to the sun, it overheats, and the frozen gas and ice turn straight into gas. This process is called sublimation and causes the comet to fizzle out.

Radiation from the sun makes the tail glow a beautiful blue-white color.

In ancient Greek, "comet" means "head with long hair."

Speeding comet

A comet knocked out of the Kuiper Belt will start to speed toward the sun. As it gets closer, it heats up, and the frozen gases and water turn back into gas, creating a small atmosphere called a coma. This coma gets pushed back by a stream of material from the sun called the solar wind, forming the tail of the comet.

See also
Find out more about the solar system (14–15).

Earth

Our home, planet Earth, is in a state of constant change. Rivers and glaciers sculpt Earth's landscape, while molten rock bubbles deep below the surface. Over millions and even billions of years, oceans open up and continents collide, shaping the surface of the Earth. Volcanoes erupt and die out, and mountains rise up and are eroded away.

Continents

The Earth today is made up of seven continents. They lie on huge slabs of rock called tectonic plates that are constantly moving. Hundreds of millions of years ago, there was just one massive stretch of land on Earth. Over time, as the plates either crashed into each other or broke apart, the land separated to form continents.

South America and Africa drifted apart as the Atlantic Ocean started to open up.

India started to drift toward Asia.

Part of the ancient Tethys Ocean between Africa, Europe, and Asia eventually became the Mediterranean Sea.

One continent

Roughly 320–200 million years ago, there was a single area of land called Pangaea. This giant landmass, or supercontinent, was surrounded by ocean.

Pangaea

Fossils Geologists studying fossilized plants and animals found similarities between those in South America and Africa. This helped them figure out that they once lived together on a supercontinent.

The Rockies This spectacular mountain range in North America was formed by Pacific Ocean plates sliding under the continental North American plate.

Breaking up

About 175 million years ago, hot, melted rock, called magma, began to rise up from within the Earth into the land above. This caused Pangaea to split up, or rift, into smaller continents.

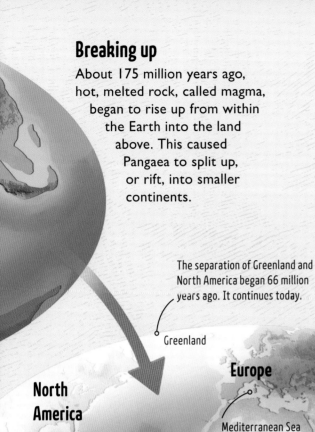

The Atlantic Ocean will continue to widen.

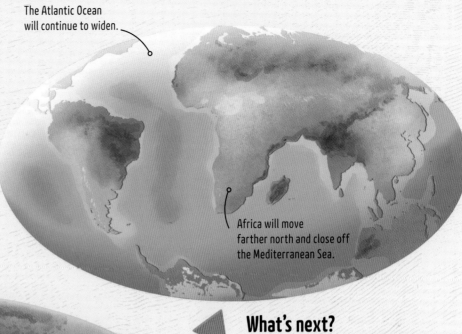

Africa will move farther north and close off the Mediterranean Sea.

The separation of Greenland and North America began 66 million years ago. It continues today.

Greenland

Europe

North America

Mediterranean Sea

Asia

India

Africa

South America

Australasia

After separating from South America, Antarctica started to become covered in ice roughly 34 million years ago.

Antarctica

What's next?

By studying the movement of the Earth's plates, geologists can predict what continents will look like 50 million years into the future.

See also
To find out more about what happens when two continents collide, see mountains (28–29).

Seven continents

The continents we have today were roughly in place about 20 million years ago. However, they are gradually and continually moving in different directions.

The Atlantic Ocean is growing at the same speed as your fingernail!

Mid-Atlantic Ridge

This ridge separates the Eurasian plate (under Europe and Asia) from the North American plate. Most of it is underwater, but in Iceland, parts of the ridge can be clearly seen.

Earthquakes
These huge tremblings of the ground happen when plates collide or slide past each other suddenly. Earthquakes can destroy buildings and kill many people.

Reaching the surface

Magma that reaches the Earth's surface is called lava. It cools quickly and solidifies into other types of igneous rock, such as basalt. Eventually, the rocks are eroded by the weather and taken toward the sea, and the rock cycle begins again.

Rain, wind, and frost

Stormy clouds carry rain, sleet, and snow that over time cause rock to weaken and break up. Windy weather also helps break up rocks.

Ice in glaciers melts into rivers and streams that carry pieces of rock to the sea.

Magma can also cool and slowly become solid underground. This creates some types of igneous rock, such as granite.

Wearing away

Rocks are carried away by a river, glacier, or winds and are gradually broken up into smaller pieces.

Magma

If the heat is very intense, sedimentary and metamorphic rocks can turn into hot liquid rock, called magma. This can burst through the surface in a volcanic eruption.

Beaches are created when tiny broken pieces of rock build up at the coast.

Heat and pressure

When sedimentary rock travels deep inside the Earth, it is put under a lot of pressure and reaches temperatures of about 400°F (200°C). This heat and pressure turn it into metamorphic rock.

Sedimentary rock changes to become metamorphic at depths of roughly 6 miles (10 km) below Earth's surface.

Rock

Rocks are made of one or more minerals. They don't look like they could travel very far on their own, but they do! Rocks move through the Earth, making their way from the surface to deep down under our feet, and returning back up again. Along the way, over millions of years, they go through huge changes.

On the beach

Over time, rock pieces settle as sand, mud, or pebbles on the coast. Usually, they get carried into the sea by rivers and settle on the seabed. Sometimes, they remain on land and compress and solidify into solid rock.

See also
Find out more about how rocks form in continents (22–23) and volcanoes (30–31).

Under the sea

Gradually, tiny pieces of rock on the seabed pile on top of each other and stick together. When the rocks compact in this way, they form sedimentary rocks.

Some pieces of sedimentary rock are dragged down farther inside the Earth.

Sedimentary Colorful bands of layered sedimentary rock are found in Badlands National Park in South Dakota.

Igneous Obsidian is an igneous rock that formed thousands of years ago when lava cooled quickly at the Earth's surface. Broken pieces of obsidian have very sharp edges.

Metamorphic Schist is a metamorphic rock that was once shale or mudstone. It is made of layers of minerals that have been folded and crumpled, which you can see in the bands of colors.

Fossil

Fossils are the preserved remains or traces of ancient animals and plants. Studying fossils helps us understand how organisms lived and evolved over time. Fossils are rare, because they form only in certain conditions over a long period of time.

Death and burial

Dying is probably the most important step in becoming fossilized! A fossil can only form if the dead animal or plant is buried quickly, because this helps slow its decay. Many fossils are formed in and around water, where remains soon sink into mud or a sandy bed.

This Stegosaurus was probably washed into the water by a high tide or flood.

Layers of rock

Tiny pieces of rock and minerals, called sediment, build up on top of the dead animal. Over time, these layers are squashed until they become solid rock, which presses down on the animal remains.

Sometimes the fossil is squashed, twisted, or flattened by the pressure of being buried.

Display

While some fossils are put on display in museums, many are never seen by the public. These hidden treasures are studied by scientists called paleontologists.

Coprolite

Coprolites are fossilized poop. The largest coprolite ever found is thought to have belonged to a T. rex and is more than 3 ft (1 m) long. Luckily, it doesn't smell anymore.

Turning to rock

Over time, the minerals that make up the remains of an animal will be completely or partially replaced by rock minerals. It is now a fossil.

Digging it up

Paleontologists use tools such as hammers and pickaxes, and even dental tools and paintbrushes, to uncover and clean a fossil.

See also
Find out more about how rocks erode in the rock cycle (24–25), and read more about dinosaurs (96–101).

Fossils are found in sedimentary rocks, such as limestone, sandstone, or mudstone, all formed by the gathering of sediment.

Erosion of the overlying rock may expose part of the fossil.

Paleontologists add plaster jackets, like the cast you get when you break a bone, to protect the fossils.

Amber This special type of fossil is formed from resin in trees. Insects and other small animals trapped in this sticky substance are perfectly preserved when it hardens.

Trace fossils Types of trace fossils include footprints, burrows, and coprolites. They can tell us more about how an animal lived and behaved than body fossils such as bones and shells.

Growing up

Young mountains rise up as long as tectonic plates continue to move into each other. The Indian plate is still moving into the Eurasian plate today, at a rate of about 2 in (5 cm) per year, and so the Himalayan mountain range at the boundary is getting higher.

When mountains form, very old rocks that were once buried deep within the Earth surge high above sea level.

Earth's crust thickens and folds to form a mountain range.

Making mountains

Tectonic plates that drift on the surface of the Earth sometimes collide with one another. When this happens, mountains, such as the Himalayas in Asia, are pushed up between them.

The rocks at the edges of continents crumple up and rise, forming mountains.

Mountain

Mountains are found on all continents and at the bottom of every ocean. They may form when two tectonic plates collide or when one plate moves under another one. Mountains don't last forever. It seems odd to imagine a mountain disappearing, but it is happening all the time.

Worn down

From the moment a mountain begins to form, it also starts to be worn away. Rain and wind break up rocks in the mountains, and rivers carry them downstream.

The Andes

Not all mountains are formed from the collision of two tectonic plates. Some form when one plate is dragged down under another one. This is how the Andes in South America were formed.

See also
Learn more about continents (22–23) and rivers (36–37).

Summits in space

Mountains are not found just on Earth, but also on the moon and some planets. A mountain called Maxwell Montes on Venus is about 7 miles (11 km) high.

Winding rivers can help carve rocks into high ridges or hills.

Flattening out

Over time, mountains disappear—as rivers, rain, and wind erode the rock and carry it to the sea. Erosion eventually flattens mountains into vast areas of flat land, called plains.

Marine mountaineers

Many mountaintops are made of rocks that originally formed in ancient oceans! These rocks contain fossils of marine animals, such as ammonites—extinct relatives of the squid.

Mount Everest is the
highest mountain on Earth.
It is 29,029 ft (8,848 m) high.

Volcano

Volcanoes can look like steep cones or have gentler slopes. They might create loud, spectacular eruptions or slow and quiet lava flows. Active volcanoes erupt regularly, although predicting exactly when this will happen is difficult. There are about 1,500 potentially active volcanoes worldwide.

During an explosive eruption, ash is launched high into the air before falling back to Earth.

The ash and magma harden into layers on the sides of the volcano, building a cone shape.

One plate sinks under another.

Magma collects in underground chambers and rises, because it is less dense than solid rock.

Magma rises through chimneys that lead to openings in the Earth's crust, known as vents. A volcano can have several vents.

Coming to life

Volcanoes usually form at the edges of Earth's massive, moving tectonic plates. When two plates collide, one plate might slide under another. Magma, ash, and gases then rise up through the Earth's interior and reach the surface, creating a volcano.

Explosive eruptions

Pressure from expanding gases inside the magma chamber slowly builds up over time, before suddenly being released during an eruption. Just how explosive an eruption will be depends on the amount of gas in the magma. Magma that is sticky and full of gas typically causes violently explosive eruptions.

Volcanoes are powered by chambers deep inside the Earth that fill up with magma.

Red-hot lava
In Hawaii, volcanic lava flows can reach temperatures of 2,147°F (1,175°C) and speeds of 20 mph (30 kph). At this temperature, lava glows bright red.

Underwater pillows

Hot lava that erupts from cracks on the sea floor solidifies very quickly into puffy round shapes. These lumps are known as pillow lavas.

Extinction

Eventually, the magma chamber below the surface empties out. No more eruptions take place, and the volcano is said to be extinct. It will be eroded away just like any other mountain.

Sleeping volcanoes

When a volcano has not erupted for decades but is expected to erupt in the future, it is said to be dormant. Some volcanoes stay dormant for centuries.

Magma that reaches the Earth's surface is called lava. It cools as it flows out of the volcano.

Over time, magma chambers start to empty out.

See also
To learn more about Earth's plates and how they move, see continents (22–23) and mountains (28–29).

Giant's Causeway

When lava cools down, it can form perfect geometrical shapes, including six-sided columns. A spectacular example of this is the Giant's Causeway in Northern Ireland.

Pompeii
In 79 CE, the deadly eruption of Mount Vesuvius in Italy destroyed the city of Pompeii. The remains of the people who lived there are preserved in hardened volcanic ash.

Creating clouds

As the water vapor rises, it cools and turns back into tiny water droplets, in a process called condensation. The droplets are so small they float in the air and form clouds.

The water cycle is powered by the sun's energy.

Water falls as rain, hail, or snow.

Rising up from the sea

Heat from the sun causes water at the ocean's surface to evaporate. This means the water turns into an invisible gas called water vapor. The vapor rises up into Earth's atmosphere.

Moisture from plants

Plants suck up water through their roots and release it as water vapor from their leaves. This adds more moisture to the air and forms more clouds.

See also
Find out how rivers form (36–37), and discover the life cycle of an iceberg (38–39).

Water

The amount of water on planet Earth never changes—it gets recycled and is used again and again. Water is always moving between the sea, the air, and the land, in a never-ending cycle. This process is called the water cycle.

Water loses its saltiness when it rises from the sea.

Rain falls

When clouds hold a lot of tiny water droplets, eventually the droplets fall as rain or, when it's colder, snow.

Some rain seeps underground through tiny cracks in rocks and makes its way to the sea.

Surface water runoff

The water from rain or melted snow that does not soak into the ground runs downhill over the surface of the land until it joins streams and rivers. It can still seep into the ground or evaporate, but most water eventually flows into the sea.

Fog Clouds don't always form up in the sky—they can also form when warm, moist air cools just above the ground or the sea. This is called fog.

Salt pans People collect salt from the sea by digging shallow pits by the shore and filling them with salty seawater. When the water evaporates, it leaves behind the salt. These pits are called salt pans.

Dry land There are some areas, such as deserts, that have very little rainfall. The driest place on Earth is the McMurdo Dry Valleys of Antarctica. Some parts haven't seen rain for nearly two million years.

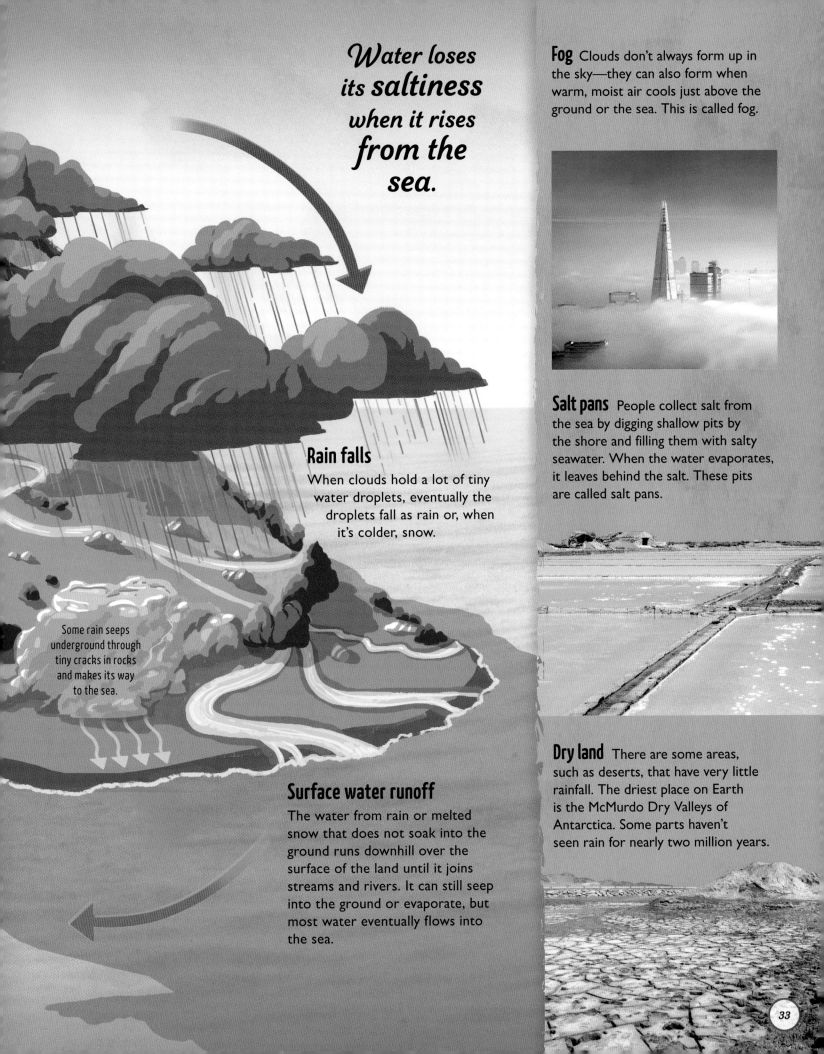

Stormy swirls

Most tornadoes develop from thunderstorms. Warm, moist air rises from the ground and meets cool, dry air, which is spinning around inside stormy clouds. A swirling column of air starts to form and extends toward the ground.

Large storms commonly have two swirling masses of air inside them. One twists clockwise, and the other counterclockwise.

A tornado can be up to 1 mile (1.6 k) high.

Tornadoes can be funnel shapes or thin rope-like shapes.

See also
To find out more about the weather, see the water cycle (32–33).

Speeding up

As warm air rises, the pressure inside the thunderstorm drops, and the swirling air speeds up. Air in a tornado can blow faster than 164 ft (50 m) per second.

Debris is swept up and violently thrown back out. Houses and trees are ripped apart.

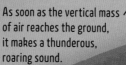

As soon as the vertical mass of air reaches the ground, it makes a thunderous, roaring sound.

Tornado

Also called twisters, tornadoes are small but extremely violent spiraling windstorms. A narrow, rotating column of air extends down from the clouds, sucks up whatever lies in its path, and leaves a trail of destruction on the ground.

Thunderstorms
Tornadoes come from cumulonimbus, or thunderstorm, clouds. These clouds are dense and towering, and they also produce rain, hail, and lightning.

Mysterious end

It is difficult to predict the direction a tornado will travel. After a few minutes, most tornadoes disappear, although some can last more than an hour before new air stops being supplied, and they die away. It remains a mystery exactly how tornadoes end their life cycle.

Dust devils
These swirling plumes of dust develop from light desert breezes. They are not as powerful as tornadoes, but can still be dangerous.

*Tornadoes contain some of the **highest wind speeds** ever recorded, at more than 300 mph (482 kph).*

Hurricanes
These huge storms form over warm ocean waters. They have an area of calm in the center, which is called the eye.

A sheltered room in a sturdy house or a storm cellar can protect people and animals.

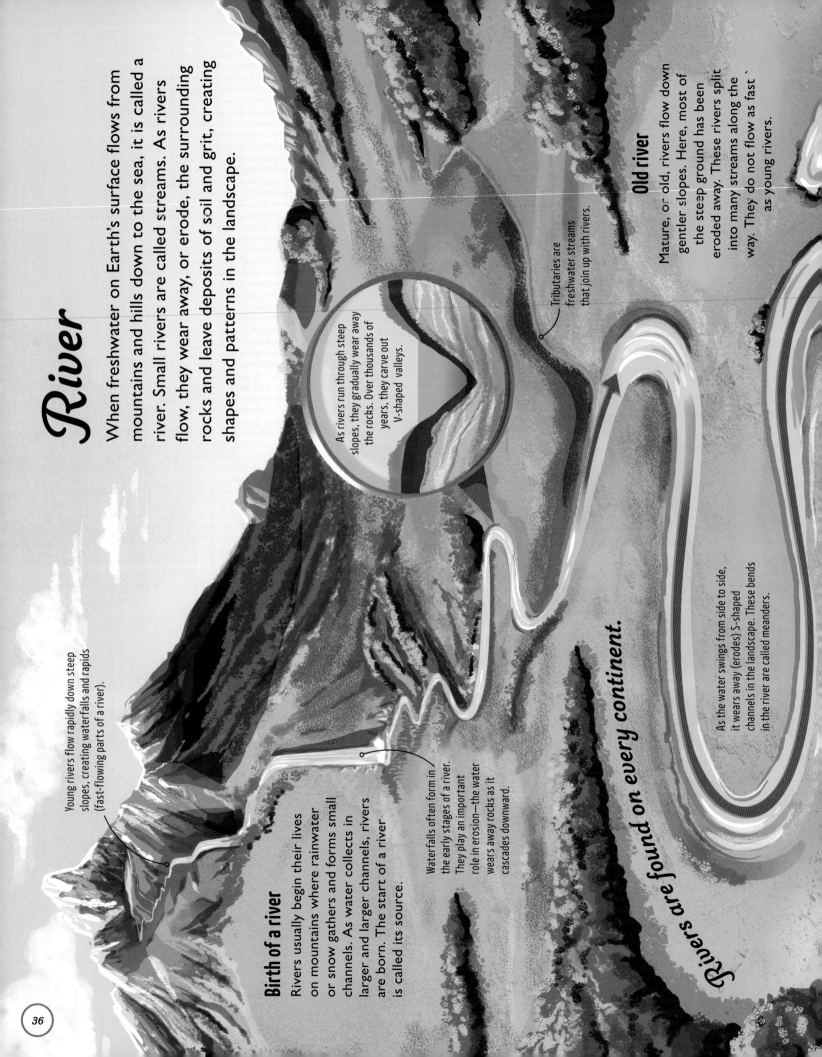

River

When freshwater on Earth's surface flows from mountains and hills down to the sea, it is called a river. Small rivers are called streams. As rivers flow, they wear away, or erode, the surrounding rocks and leave deposits of soil and grit, creating shapes and patterns in the landscape.

Young rivers flow rapidly down steep slopes, creating waterfalls and rapids (fast-flowing parts of a river).

As rivers run through steep slopes, they gradually wear away the rocks. Over thousands of years, they carve out V-shaped valleys.

Tributaries are freshwater streams that join up with rivers.

Old river

Mature, or old, rivers flow down gentler slopes. Here, most of the steep ground has been eroded away. These rivers split into many streams along the way. They do not flow as fast as young rivers.

Birth of a river

Rivers usually begin their lives on mountains where rainwater or snow gathers and forms small channels. As water collects in larger and larger channels, rivers are born. The start of a river is called its source.

Waterfalls often form in the early stages of a river. They play an important role in erosion—the water wears away rocks as it cascades downward.

Rivers are found on every continent.

As the water swings from side to side, it wears away (erodes) S-shaped channels in the landscape. These bends in the river are called meanders.

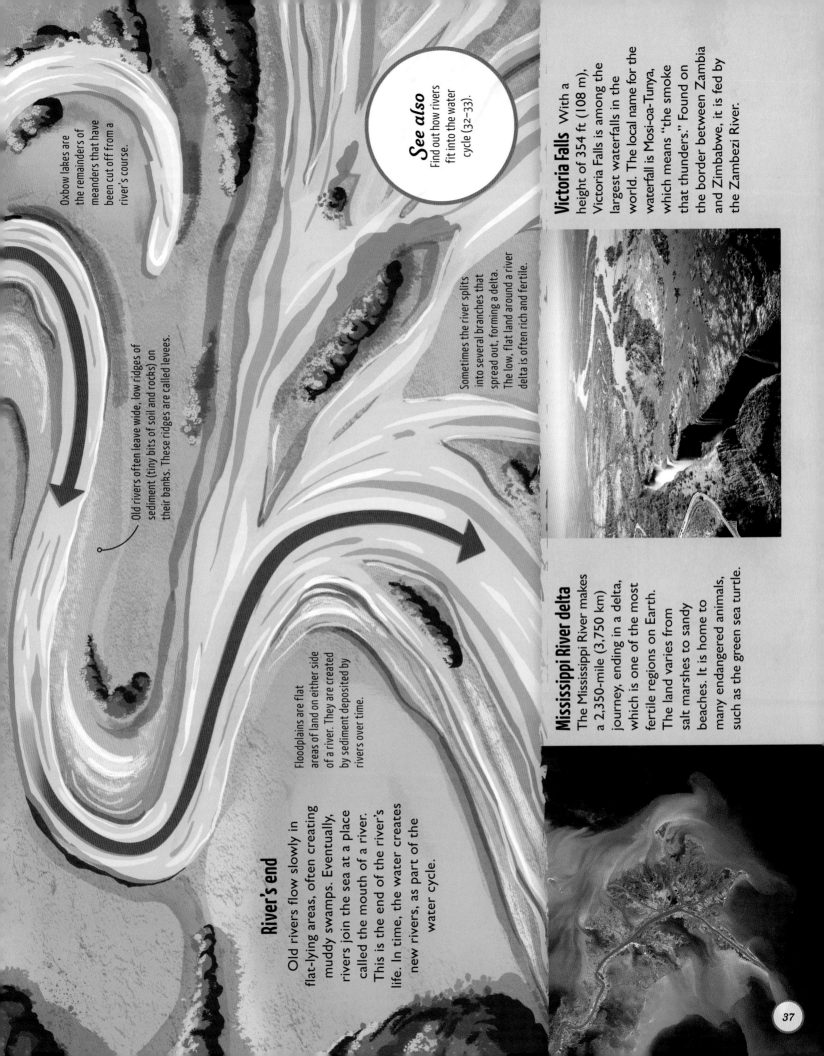

Oxbow lakes are the remainders of meanders that have been cut off from a river's course.

Old rivers often leave wide, low ridges of sediment (tiny bits of soil and rocks) on their banks. These ridges are called levees.

Sometimes the river splits into several branches that spread out, forming a delta. The low, flat land around a river delta is often rich and fertile.

See also

Find out how rivers fit into the water cycle (32–33).

River's end

Old rivers flow slowly in flat-lying areas, often creating muddy swamps. Eventually, rivers join the sea at a place called the mouth of a river. This is the end of the river's life. In time, the water creates new rivers, as part of the water cycle.

Floodplains are flat areas of land on either side of a river. They are created by sediment deposited by rivers over time.

Victoria Falls

With a height of 354 ft (108 m), Victoria Falls is among the largest waterfalls in the world. The local name for the waterfall is Mosi-oa-Tunya, which means "the smoke that thunders." Found on the border between Zambia and Zimbabwe, it is fed by the Zambezi River.

Mississippi River delta

The Mississippi River makes a 2,350-mile (3,750 km) journey, ending in a delta, which is one of the most fertile regions on Earth. The land varies from salt marshes to sandy beaches. It is home to many endangered animals, such as the green sea turtle.

Iceberg

Icebergs are large chunks of ice, found in both the Arctic and Antarctic regions. They are formed when pieces break away from glaciers—huge moving masses of ice. Icebergs change shape and even color. Many sea creatures use icebergs as hunting grounds.

Making a glacier

When snowflakes pile up and compress into tightly packed snow, a glacier is formed. Glaciers cover roughly 10 percent of the Earth's surface and store up to 75 percent of its freshwater. Glaciers move forward as ice and snow build up and then retreat backward when thawing.

See also
Find out about penguins living in the icy region of Antarctica (108–109).

Emperor penguins gather on icebergs looking for food.

Breaking free

At the glacier's edge, or terminus, chunks of ice break off into the water. This is called calving, and the chunks are now icebergs. They range in size from around 6.5 ft (2 m) long to huge slabs about the size of a small country.

Floating away

Icebergs are made of frozen freshwater, yet they float on salty ocean water. They typically last for three to six years. Carried along by the waves, icebergs can crash into one another or onto land.

Ice stripes Some icebergs are striped! These dark lines come from the bits of soil and sediment that the iceberg picked up when it broke away from the glacier.

Flat tops Icebergs can be all kinds of different shapes, including wedge shaped, dome shaped, or topped with spires. Those with flat, sheetlike tops and steep sides are called tabular icebergs, such as this rectangular iceberg that was found in Antarctica.

Shapeshifter

Waves wear away (erode) the edges of icebergs, creating spectacular arches and caves in the ice. When icebergs grind against the seabed or the shore, they can also get sculpted into different shapes.

Small bits of ice that break off the iceberg are called growlers—they can be a danger for passing ships.

Life on the iceberg

Icebergs host their own mini communities, or ecosystems, of living organisms. They attract tiny algae, krill, and fish. Seabirds, such as petrels and penguins, hunt and feed on these sea creatures.

Melting away

When icebergs drift into warmer waters or are surrounded by warm air, they start to melt. As the ice melts into pools and cracks form and widen, the iceberg slowly disappears.

Tiny sea creatures called krill make a tasty meal for penguins livng on the ice.

Colored ice Icebergs are usually white or blue, but algae living on the ice can produce a variety of colors, including green. Some icebergs are rich in iron from rock dust, resulting in a yellow or reddish color.

Only one-eighth of an iceberg floats above the ocean's surface. Most of it is underwater.

Carbon

Carbon is essential to all life on Earth. It is in the atmosphere, oceans, plants, soil, rocks, and even our bodies. The total amount of carbon in the world never increases or decreases, but it is always moving around and changing form. This process is called the carbon cycle.

In the atmosphere

In the air, carbon is combined with oxygen in carbon dioxide (CO2). CO2 is known as a greenhouse gas because it traps heat. Reducing the amount of CO2 in the atmosphere helps prevent global warming.

Plants help lower the amount of carbon dioxide in the atmosphere.

Absorbing

Plants use light energy from the sun to combine carbon dioxide from the air with water to make food. This is called photosynthesis.

Dead animals and plants release CO2 when they decay.

Carbon can stay trapped at the bottom of deep oceans for thousands, or even millions, of years.

Storing

Over millions of years, dead organisms, which contain carbon, turn into fossil fuels such as coal and oil.

Rain forests Trees absorb lots of CO2, helping reduce greenhouse gas in the atmosphere. However, deforestation (cutting down lots of trees) gets in the way of this natural process.

Rocks Most of Earth's carbon—about 64 trillion tons—is stored in rocks. However, wind, rain, and ice can break down rock and release CO2 back into the ocean or atmosphere.

There is more carbon dioxide in the air today than at any time in the past 800,000 years.

See also
To learn more about people's impact on the carbon cycle, see "How we affect life on Earth" (136–137).

Burning fossil fuels releases lots of CO2.

Animals breathe out CO2 and eat plants, which contain carbon.

Releasing
Living things expel carbon dioxide through respiration (breathing). Burning fossil fuels also releases CO2. Some rocks slowly release carbon dioxide, too.

Oil rigs drill deep down into the Earth to extract oil and natural gas.

Fossil fuels build up in rocky layers buried deep below the surface.

Heating up Carbon dioxide released by humans through the burning of fossil fuels is currently warming up Earth's climate, melting ice and destroying glaciers.

Green energy Unlike fossil fuels, sources of energy such as solar panels and wind farms do not upset the carbon cycle or alter the climate. This is called green energy.

Life *on* Earth

Living things have dwelt on our planet for at least 3.5 billion years. The first life was nothing more than slimy scum made from single-celled microbes. But from these simple beginnings—and over countless generations—the world became filled with animals and plants that swarmed the oceans and turned the land green with forests.

Many Cambrian animals, such as Marrella, had long creeping legs, sort of like a crab's.

Life begins

A billion years after Earth formed, its bare rocky land and deep blue oceans would have appeared empty of life. But somewhere under the waves, single-celled organisms—bacteria—became the first life on Earth.

Water flooded across the Earth's surface, turning much of it blue.

First animals

Somewhere on the ocean floor, living things evolved to have larger bodies made up of billions of cells, so they grew much bigger than microbes. These were the very first animals—but they were unlike anything alive today.

The Cambrian explosion

During a period of time called the Cambrian, conditions were just right for lots of different kinds of ocean animals to evolve. Many would have looked similar to creatures alive today, such as jellyfish, worms, and shrimps.

Earth is formed

There was a time when the sun was surrounded by just swirling clouds of dust and rocks. Then these clumped together to form the solar system's planets, including Earth.

The egg-shaped Dickinsonia probably crawled on the ocean floor.

4.54 bya

4 bya

600 mya

540 mya

bya = billion years ago
mya = million years ago

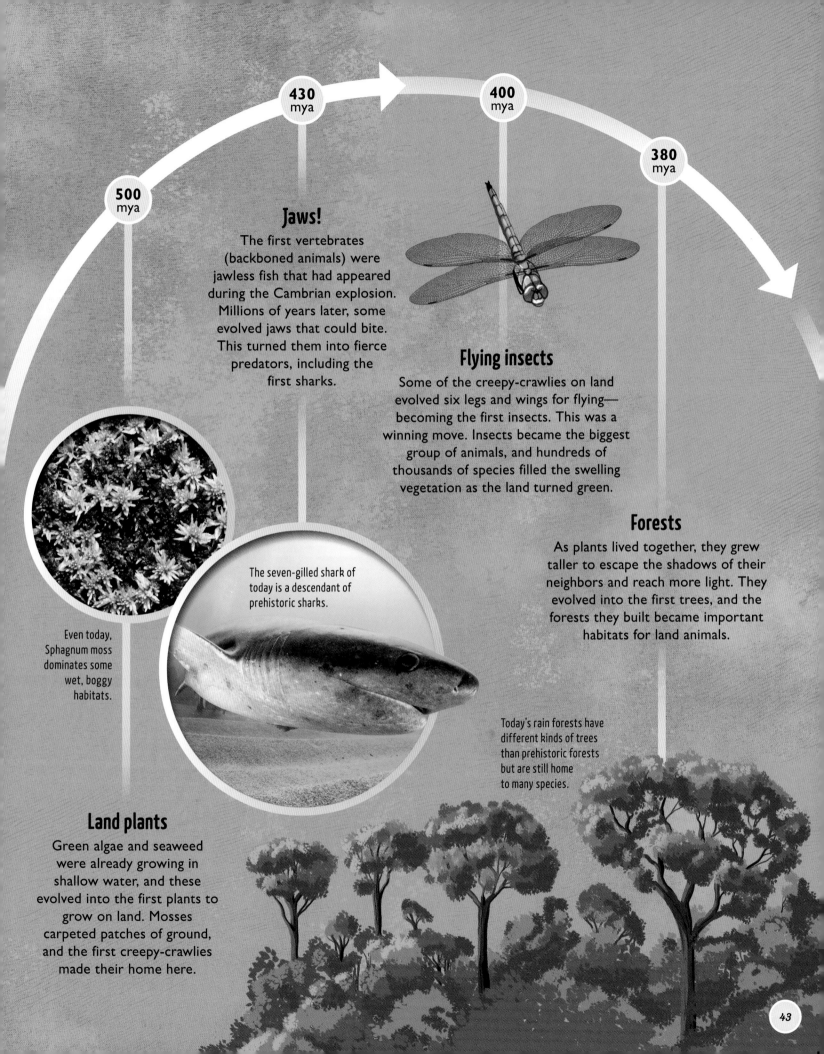

500
mya

430
mya

400
mya

380
mya

Jaws!

The first vertebrates (backboned animals) were jawless fish that had appeared during the Cambrian explosion. Millions of years later, some evolved jaws that could bite. This turned them into fierce predators, including the first sharks.

Flying insects

Some of the creepy-crawlies on land evolved six legs and wings for flying—becoming the first insects. This was a winning move. Insects became the biggest group of animals, and hundreds of thousands of species filled the swelling vegetation as the land turned green.

Forests

As plants lived together, they grew taller to escape the shadows of their neighbors and reach more light. They evolved into the first trees, and the forests they built became important habitats for land animals.

Even today, Sphagnum moss dominates some wet, boggy habitats.

The seven-gilled shark of today is a descendant of prehistoric sharks.

Today's rain forests have different kinds of trees than prehistoric forests but are still home to many species.

Land plants

Green algae and seaweed were already growing in shallow water, and these evolved into the first plants to grow on land. Mosses carpeted patches of ground, and the first creepy-crawlies made their home here.

Giant reptiles

The reptilian form was so successful that reptiles evolved into some of the most incredible animals ever to have lived. Huge ichthyosaurs swam in the seas, followed by giant dinosaurs that stalked the land.

Amphibians

Fish had evolved fins to control their swimming, but some with fleshy fins could waddle onto land. As they evolved lungs to breathe air, they became the first amphibians—distant relatives of today's salamanders and frogs.

Ichthyosaurs were shaped like today's dolphins but were reptiles, not mammals.

Flowers

For millions of years, plants on land reproduced by scattering dustlike spores on the wind or generating seeds in cones. But when the first flowers appeared, the land bloomed with color— and pollinating insects thrived on their sugary nectar.

Reptiles

Amphibians kept the moist skin of their fishy ancestors and needed to return to water to lay their soft eggs. But some evolved ways to survive for longer on land. They had dry, scaly skin and laid hard-shelled eggs, becoming the first reptiles.

Like other early mammals, Morganucodon was probably nocturnal.

Mammals

At the time of the dinosaurs, furry descendants of smaller reptiles were scurrying over the ground and living in burrows. These were evolving into the first mammals: over time, mothers gave birth to live young and nourished them with breast milk.

375 mya

Giant land tortoises first appeared a few million years ago.

320 mya

300 mya

250 mya

200 mya

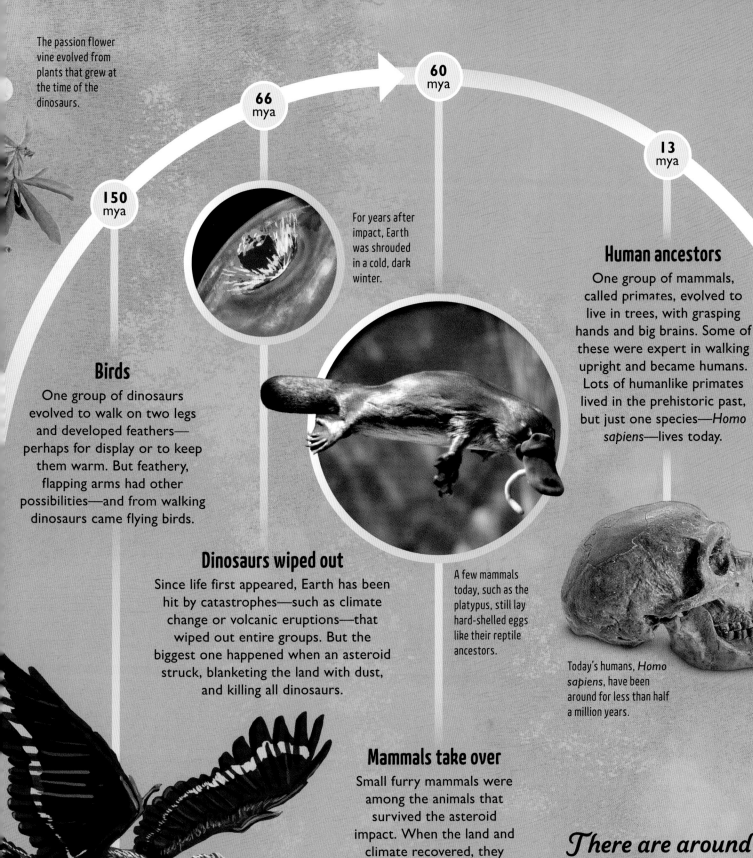

The passion flower vine evolved from plants that grew at the time of the dinosaurs.

150 mya

66 mya

60 mya

13 mya

For years after impact, Earth was shrouded in a cold, dark winter.

Birds

One group of dinosaurs evolved to walk on two legs and developed feathers—perhaps for display or to keep them warm. But feathery, flapping arms had other possibilities—and from walking dinosaurs came flying birds.

Human ancestors

One group of mammals, called primates, evolved to live in trees, with grasping hands and big brains. Some of these were expert in walking upright and became humans. Lots of humanlike primates lived in the prehistoric past, but just one species—*Homo sapiens*—lives today.

Dinosaurs wiped out

Since life first appeared, Earth has been hit by catastrophes—such as climate change or volcanic eruptions—that wiped out entire groups. But the biggest one happened when an asteroid struck, blanketing the land with dust, and killing all dinosaurs.

A few mammals today, such as the platypus, still lay hard-shelled eggs like their reptile ancestors.

Today's humans, *Homo sapiens*, have been around for less than half a million years.

Mammals take over

Small furry mammals were among the animals that survived the asteroid impact. When the land and climate recovered, they evolved to replace the dinosaurs as predatory meat eaters and grazing plant eaters.

Archaeopteryx was a prehistoric bird with feathers and a beak—but it also had reptilian teeth and claws on its wings.

There are around 1.3 million species known on Earth today, and many more yet to be discovered.

Slime mold Many types of slime mold live as single cells, like amoebas. However, some stick together to form fungus-like bodies that reproduce by releasing spores.

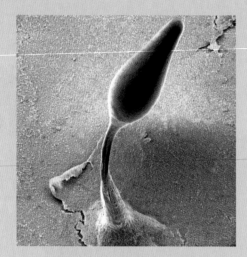

Bacteria Like amoebas, bacteria are single-celled and reproduce by dividing. However, a bacterium's cells are tinier, and its DNA is not packaged inside a nucleus.

Virus Even smaller than bacteria, viruses are little more than capsules containing genetic information, and they can reproduce only inside cells of living things.

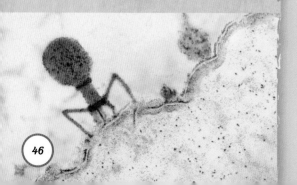

Amoeba

The single-celled amoeba is so tiny its entire life cycle can happen in a drop of water. Its one cell never grows bigger than a period on this page. However, like all cells, it is packed with everything it needs to reproduce and make more of its kind.

Each amoeba contains a special spot called a nucleus, which controls what the cell can do.

Greedy amoeba

The amoeba is a microscopic predator. It feeds on smaller single-celled creatures, such as algae. The amoeba swallows its prey by stretching out "fingers" of a clear jelly, called cytoplasm.

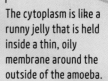

The cytoplasm is like a runny jelly that is held inside a thin, oily membrane around the outside of the amoeba.

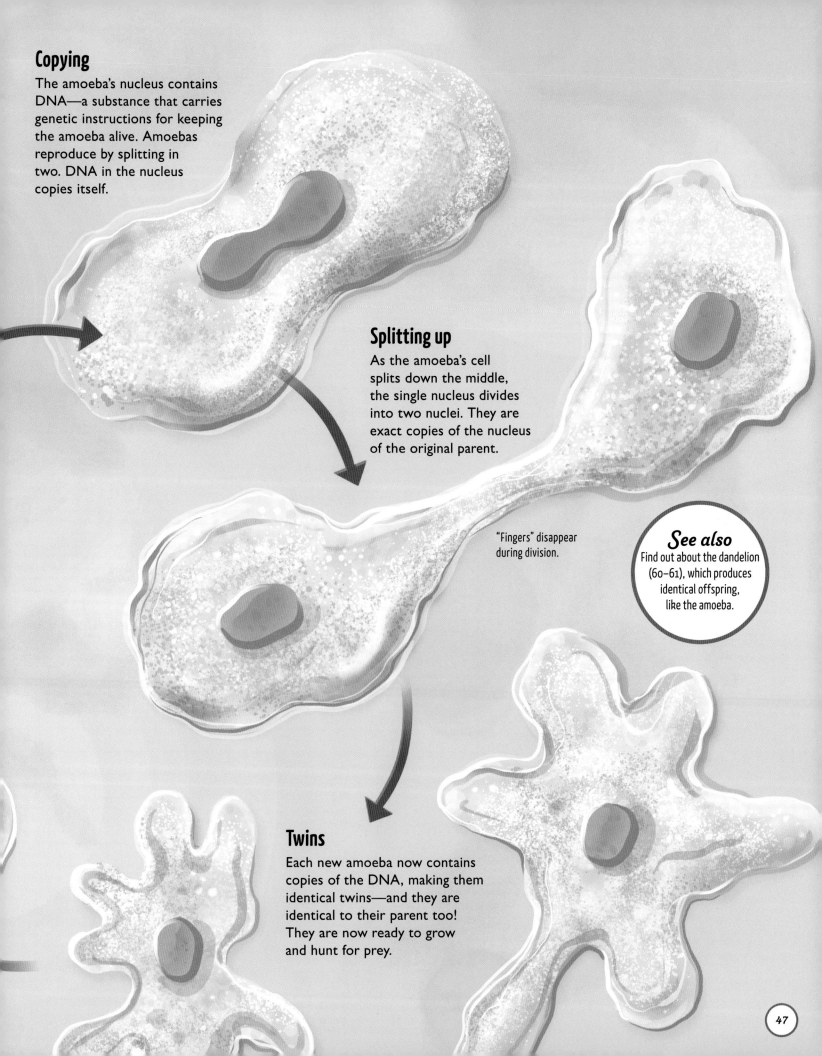

Copying

The amoeba's nucleus contains DNA—a substance that carries genetic instructions for keeping the amoeba alive. Amoebas reproduce by splitting in two. DNA in the nucleus copies itself.

Splitting up

As the amoeba's cell splits down the middle, the single nucleus divides into two nuclei. They are exact copies of the nucleus of the original parent.

"Fingers" disappear during division.

See also
Find out about the dandelion (60–61), which produces identical offspring, like the amoeba.

Twins

Each new amoeba now contains copies of the DNA, making them identical twins—and they are identical to their parent too! They are now ready to grow and hunt for prey.

Plants and Fungi

The lives of plants and fungi are anchored to the ground. Plants branch upward to catch the energy in sunshine, while fungi hug the soil to get nourishment from death and decay. But both have life cycles that take them beyond where they are rooted, because their spores or seeds scatter far and wide to germinate into a new generation.

Spores *to* seeds

Although they are rooted in the ground, plants find ways of spreading their offspring. Mosses and ferns do it by scattering dustlike spores. However, most plants do it with seeds. Inside each seed is a tiny baby plant that even comes with its own store of food. This gives it a better chance of surviving and germinating (developing) when it reaches moist ground.

Growing from seeds

Most plants produce dustlike pollen. However, unlike spores, pollen does not develop on its own but is used to fertilize the plant's eggs. Each fertilized egg then grows into a tiny plant embryo inside a seed.

Some plants, such as pine trees, produce pollen and eggs inside cones.

Mosses and ferns

The first plants to evolve on land reproduced using spores. Each dustlike spore is a tiny single cell that can germinate into a new plant. Mosses produce spores in capsules on stalks, while most ferns make spores on the underside of their leaves.

Moss spores are released from tall stalks so they are more likely to drift away on the wind.

Ferns grow clusters of tiny brown cases. As the cases dry out and split open, the spores inside burst into the air.

Most cones turn hard and woody as they mature, but the cones of junipers develop into sweet berries.

Most fern leaves unfurl from buds called fiddleheads.

Many cone-producing plants have tough needlelike leaves, but those of the monkey puzzle tree are wide and fleshy.

Flowering plants

Flowers help plants reproduce. Many have eye-catching colors, sweet scents, and tasty nectar that entice pollinating animals, such as bees. Once the seeds are fertilized, they develop inside the fruit.

The bright colors of a bird-of-paradise flower attract nectar-seeking pollinators, such as sunbirds.

Bristlecone pines grow very slowly but live long. One—thought to be more than 4,800 years old—could be one of the oldest living things on the planet.

Ripe fruits are often filled with sweet juice—perfect for attracting sugar-loving animals who, by devouring the fruit, help scatter the seeds inside.

In springtime some plants, such as magnolias, produce flowers even before they sprout leaves.

Most plants need their pollen to be carried to other flowers. However, some—such as this Antarctic pearlwort—can pollinate themselves.

There are more than 250,000 species of flowering plant.

Sunflowers

Cacti

Mushroom

Fungi are not animals and they're not plants. They are made up of masses of tiny branching threads. We usually notice them only when they produce mushrooms, which are their fruiting bodies. Poisonous mushrooms, like the colorful fly agaric mushroom, are often called toadstools—be careful never to touch or pick them.

Fly agaric mushrooms grow alone or in small clusters on the forest floor.

The bright red color of the cap warns that the fly agaric mushroom is very poisonous.

Settling

When the spores settle in new places, they germinate (sprout) and produce fine threads called hyphae. As the hyphae grow, they branch and spread out, feeding on moisture and nutrients in the soil.

The tiny, lightweight spores drift far and wide on the wind.

See also
Find out about plants that reproduce using spores (50–51).

Cloud of spores

A fly agaric mushroom releases millions of white spores, which are sort of like seeds. The spores blow away on the wind, and only a few will end up growing into new fungi.

Birch tree
The fly agaric often grows near birch trees. The hyphae wrap around tree roots and supply the trees with nutrients from the soil. In return, the fungus receives sugars made in the trees' leaves.

Devil's fingers
This creepy fungus is covered in gooey slime that smells like rotting flesh. The slime contains the spores of the fungus. Beetles, flies, and slugs attracted by the fumes get covered in slime and carry off the spores when they leave.

Baby mushroom

A young mushroom is protected by a special white coat called a veil. As the cap gets bigger, the veil breaks. The white, warty spots on the red cap are the remains of the veil.

The white coat is called a veil.

The young mushroom develops a cap, which is pushed up from the soil on a stalk.

The tiny knots develop into mushrooms.

Spores fall from flaps under the cap. The flaps look like fish gills.

Mat of threads

The hyphae spread out through the soil, weaving together into a mat of threads called a mycelium. The mycelium is the main part of the fungus. It feeds by taking in nutrients from dead plant and animal matter in the soil.

Knots and pinheads

When it's time to reproduce, the hyphae from different fungi knot together and form clumps in the mycelium. The knots get larger and can be seen as tiny white "pinheads" on the surface of the soil. These pinheads will become young mushrooms.

Mature mushroom

Scientists call the fully grown mushroom a fruiting body. Its cap and stalk are made of hyphae packed tightly together. Underneath the cap are papery flaps called gills. Spores line the surface of the gills.

Puffball The puffball fungus has a ball-shaped top, which is its fruiting body. It releases its spores inside the ball. When the mushroom is knocked by animals or hit by raindrops, it splits, and a cloud of spores puffs out.

Forest cleaners Fungi are waste disposal experts. As they feed, they help dead plants and animals rot and decay (decompose). Without fungi, forests would become buried by the remains of dead organisms.

Giant sequoia

The tallest living thing on Earth, the giant sequoia tree is as high as a 26-story building, and wider than the average city street. Found only in western California, these incredible trees can live for thousands of years. Even after death, they continue to support life.

New life

The life of the giant sequoia springs from its cones. Pollen from the male cones is blown on the wind to fertilize eggs in the female cones, producing seeds.

Bursting out

Seeds spread when the cones split open. This might be thanks to a hungry squirrel feeding on the cones. However, more often it is due to the cones drying out from the heat from a forest fire, causing them to split.

Young or old?

For the first 250 years, the tree is still considered to be young! In these early years, branches grow from near the base of the trunk as well as from the top. Its leaves are evergreen—they stay on the tree all year round.

Tender plant

The seed grows into a young plant called a seedling. The tree starts to produce cones when it is 10 years old and continues producing them into old age.

See also
Read more about seeds and pollination in the coconut tree (56–57) and the oak tree (62–63).

20 years old   100 years old   200 years old

54

Grown-up tree

The tree has reached full height when it's between 500 and 750 years old. By this time, it has also changed shape. While the top of the trunk is laden with branches, the lower part has none. The tree can survive for more than 2,500 years.

Under threat
Despite their thick bark, giant sequoias can be destroyed by disease or forest fires spreading between their branches. It takes a long time for giant sequoias to reproduce, and other, faster-growing trees can take their place in the forest.

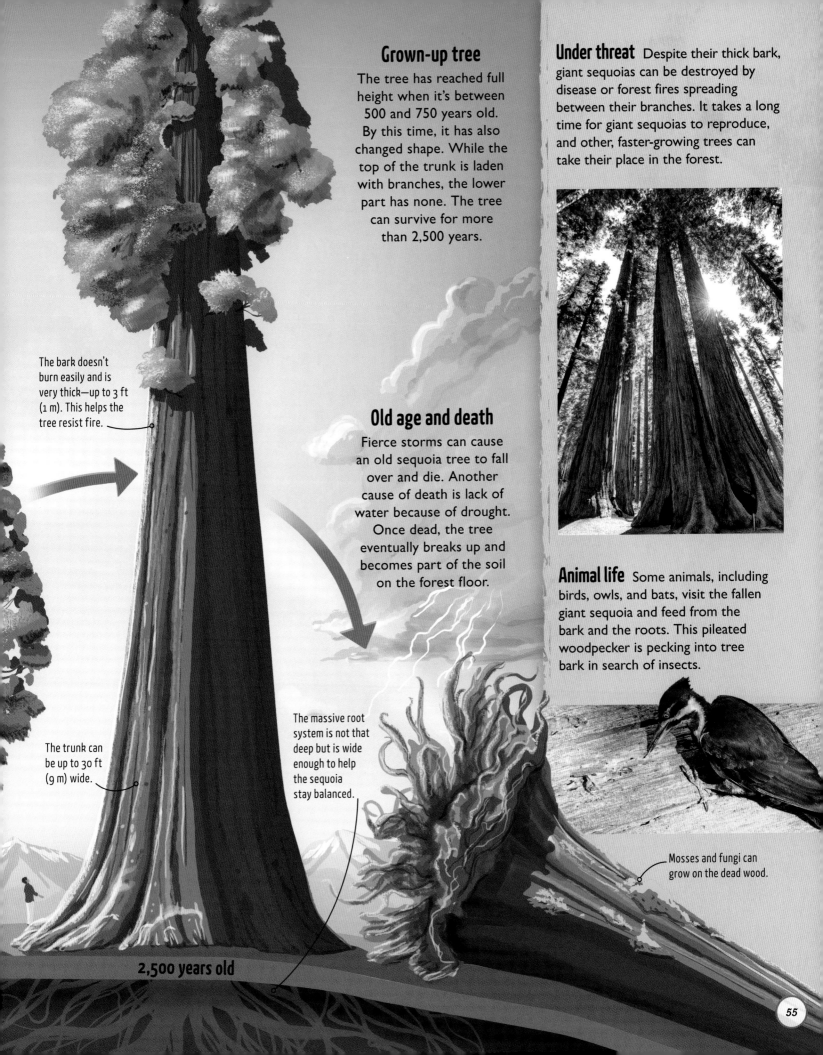

The bark doesn't burn easily and is very thick—up to 3 ft (1 m). This helps the tree resist fire.

Old age and death

Fierce storms can cause an old sequoia tree to fall over and die. Another cause of death is lack of water because of drought. Once dead, the tree eventually breaks up and becomes part of the soil on the forest floor.

Animal life
Some animals, including birds, owls, and bats, visit the fallen giant sequoia and feed from the bark and the roots. This pileated woodpecker is pecking into tree bark in search of insects.

The massive root system is not that deep but is wide enough to help the sequoia stay balanced.

The trunk can be up to 30 ft (9 m) wide.

Mosses and fungi can grow on the dead wood.

2,500 years old

The yellow flowers bloom all year round.

Flowering

The tree produces flowers when it is around seven years old. Insects feed on the sweet nectar and pollinate the flowers, which then develop into fruits.

Growing up

By the time it is 20 years old, the coconut palm is fully grown and 100 ft (30 m) tall. Up to 40 feather-like leaves, called fronds, grow in a "crown" from a single bud at the top of the trunk.

Young fruit

Coconuts start off as green fruit and take about a year to ripen on the tree. Eventually, their stems break, and the heavy fruits fall to the ground. The coconut seed is hidden inside the fruit. Some germinate where they fall, while others are carried off by the waves.

Coconut palm

A coconut palm's seeds are contained in its coconuts. The seeds are spread not by air or on the backs of animals, but with the help of the sea. Coconuts are often washed into the water and then drift on ocean currents to beaches far away.

Tough drupe

The coconut fruit is called a drupe. Beneath its smooth skin is a thick brown husk made of fibers. The husk surrounds a single seed.

As the drupe breaks open, shoots and roots grow from the coconut seed.

The drupe floats thanks to air trapped in the husk. Protective layers keep it from being damaged by seawater.

Most of the roots are shallow—only a few go deeper. New roots grow throughout the tree's life, and adult palms may have up to 7,000.

Roots and shoots

The white flesh and water inside the coconut provide food and moisture for the sprouting seed. A single shoot grows upward, while roots reach down into the soil.

See also

Find out about the dandelion (60–61), whose seeds are spread by the wind, and the orchid (58–59) and oak tree (62–63), whose seeds are spread by animals.

Drupe Mango and peach trees also bear fruit called drupes. These fruits have a fleshy layer that surrounds a hard, woody shell, or "stone," that contains the seed. Coconuts have a hard husk instead of a fleshy layer.

Palm oil Another type of palm tree—the oil palm—bears a fruit that produces oil. The oil is used to make many things, from chocolate to toothpaste. However, there is a problem: forests are being cut down to make way for oil palms, and endangered animals such as orangutans are losing their homes.

57

Orchid

Many flowers rely on sweet nectar to attract pollinating animals. Bucket orchids are different. They are pollinated only by male euglossine bees (also known as orchid bees). The orchids attract the bees with a unique scent. When the bee visit the flowers, the blooms get pollinated—in return, the bee picks up a scent that helps it find a mate.

Treetop flower

The bucket orchid grows in nests made by ants on the branches of forest trees. The ants feed on the orchid's sweet nectar, while the plant's roots take nutrients from the nest. Soon, the orchid produces an unusually shaped flower.

The male bee recognizes the bucket orchid's unique scent.

Collecting scent

The scent of bucket orchid flowers attracts only euglossine bees. When a bee arrives, he collects the fragrance and stores it in special "perfume pouches" on his back legs.

The scent is produced under the flower's "hood."

The pollen packets are stuck to the bee's back, out of his reach.

See also
Read about how the rafflesia flower (66–67) uses its foul stink, rather than a sweet perfume, to attract flies.

Splash down

The flower's surface is slippery, and the bee soon falls into a goo-filled bowl at the flower's base. Luckily, there's an escape route—a tube just wide enough for the euglossine bee.

Wriggling out

As the bee tries to wriggle out, the tube tightens and traps him. Two packets of pollen are stuck to the bee with a kind of quick-drying glue.

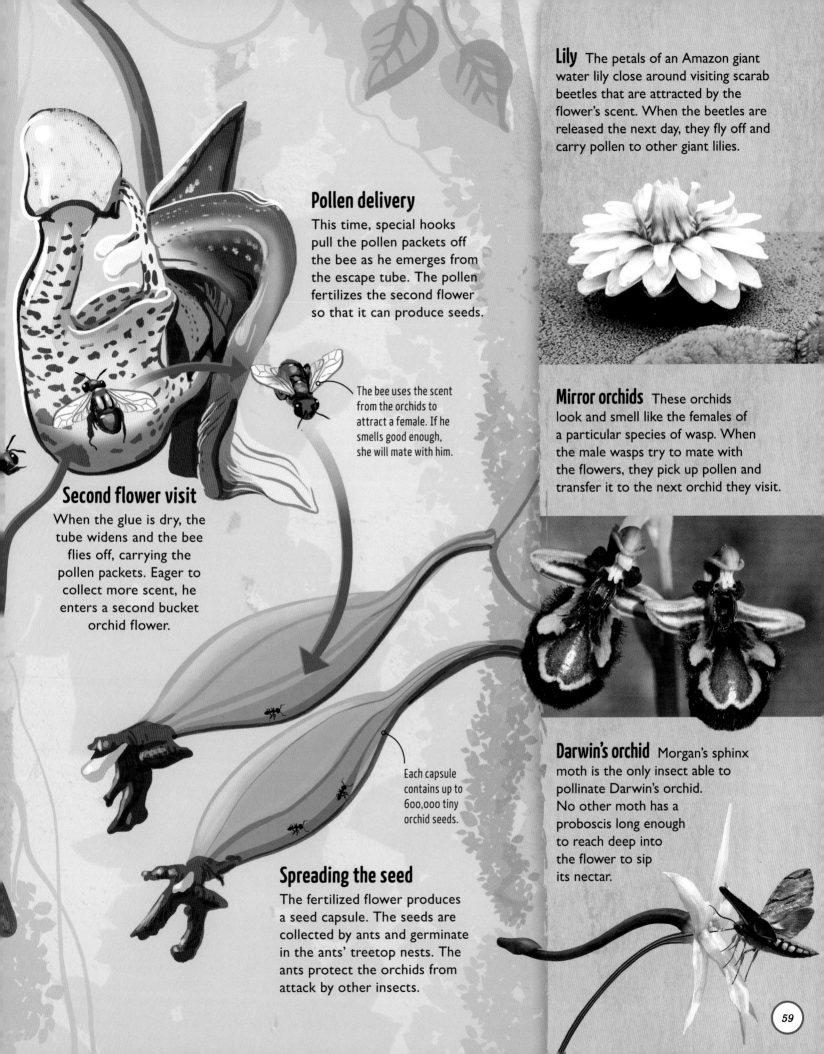

Pollen delivery

This time, special hooks pull the pollen packets off the bee as he emerges from the escape tube. The pollen fertilizes the second flower so that it can produce seeds.

The bee uses the scent from the orchids to attract a female. If he smells good enough, she will mate with him.

Second flower visit

When the glue is dry, the tube widens and the bee flies off, carrying the pollen packets. Eager to collect more scent, he enters a second bucket orchid flower.

Each capsule contains up to 600,000 tiny orchid seeds.

Spreading the seed

The fertilized flower produces a seed capsule. The seeds are collected by ants and germinate in the ants' treetop nests. The ants protect the orchids from attack by other insects.

Lily The petals of an Amazon giant water lily close around visiting scarab beetles that are attracted by the flower's scent. When the beetles are released the next day, they fly off and carry pollen to other giant lilies.

Mirror orchids These orchids look and smell like the females of a particular species of wasp. When the male wasps try to mate with the flowers, they pick up pollen and transfer it to the next orchid they visit.

Darwin's orchid Morgan's sphinx moth is the only insect able to pollinate Darwin's orchid. No other moth has a proboscis long enough to reach deep into the flower to sip its nectar.

59

Insects arrive to gather pollen and nectar, but the plant doesn't need them to make seeds.

Blossoming

Flower heads appear at the ends of long stems. Each head is actually a cluster of many small petal-shaped flowers called ray florets. Every ray floret can form a seed.

Dandelion

Unlike many flowering plants, dandelions usually make seeds without being pollinated. This is known as asexual reproduction. However, insects still visit dandelions to collect pollen and nectar. A relationship like this, in which one partner (the insect) is helped and the other (the dandelion) is unaffected, is called commensalism.

Spring growth

In spring, leaves sprout from the plant's main root, called a taproot, which has survived the winter underground. The root goes deep into the soil to get water and nutrients to feed the plant.

House mouse Like dandelions and insects, humans and mice have a commensal relationship—one partner benefits and the other doesn't. Mice find shelter and food in our homes. Apart from their droppings and gnawings, they cause us little bother, although they can carry disease.

Seed heads

When flowering has finished, a puffy white seed head develops, full of seeds. A light breeze is all that's needed to blow the seeds away.

Each seed is attached by a stalk to a "parachute" that helps it drift on the wind.

Spreading seeds

Most seeds land close to the plant they came from—the parent plant. Other seeds travel on the wind far away. The seeds of unpollinated flowers grow into new plants. These are copies, or clones, of the parent plant.

See also
Find out about flowering plants that must always be pollinated to make seeds—orchids (58–59) and oaks (62–63).

The delicate parachute is actually a tuft of around 100 threadlike hairs.

Remora This fish has a sucker on its head that lets it attach itself harmlessly to bigger sea creatures, such as a shark. The remora gets a free ride, protection, and food scraps from the shark.

Pseudoscorpion These tiny creatures are related to scorpions. They hitch a ride by clinging to flying insects. This doesn't harm the insects, and the pseudoscorpions get to travel much farther than they could on their own.

See also
Find out about evergreen trees, such as the giant sequoia (54–55) and coconut palm (56–57).

The upper parts of the tree are now buzzing with summer insects.

Male oak flowers, which produce pollen, hang in long tassels called catkins. Female flowers, which are harder to spot, grow in small clusters.

The female flower is fertilized by windblown pollen and forms an acorn, which is held in a protective woody cup.

Spring

While resting through winter, the oak has been saving its energy for spring. As the days grow warmer and longer, new green leaves grow from buds on the branches, and the tree flowers. Oaks have both male and female flowers.

Summer

During the long, hot days, leaves use sunlight to make food for the tree. This process is photosynthesis. The acorns formed by the flowers ripen in late summer. Acorns are a type of hard-shelled fruit called nuts.

Spreading seeds Most acorns are eaten before they can germinate. However, animals that eat acorns help oaks spread to new places, too. Squirrels bury acorns to store them for winter, but they sometimes forget where they left them. Birds may accidentally drop acorns in midflight. The forgotten acorns may then grow into new trees, away from the parent oak.

Oak

An oak is more than just a tree—it is home to as many as 350 species of insect and many other animals. Oaks and other deciduous trees change with the seasons. The oak's seeds are found in fruits called acorns. A single oak tree can produce 90,000 acorns a year.

When ripe, acorns break off their stalks and fall to the ground. Each acorn contains a seed that can grow into a new tree.

Fall

Fall winds blow the acorns off the tree. As the days get cooler and shorter, the tree prepares for winter. Its green leaves turn to shades of yellow, orange, and red, before dropping to the ground.

Winter

Winter days are cold and short. Although the oak looks dead, with its branches bare of leaves, it is actually still alive. The tree is in dormancy, which is like a winter sleep.

Fungus Eventually, an old oak will be invaded by fungi, which cause it to decay. The weakened trunk may then break under the weight of the branches above or by the force of the wind.

Deciduous Like the oak, this cherry tree is deciduous—it sheds its leaves each fall and grows new leaves in spring, along with pink blossoms. Trees that keep their leaves all year round, such as pine trees, are called evergreens.

Catching food

There are tiny hairs on the surface of the trap that are sensitive to touch. If the fly touches the hairs twice within 20 seconds, the trap snaps shut. The plant eats the fly's soft body parts and absorbs the nutrients. When the trap reopens, the remains blow away on the wind or are washed away by rain.

The fly touches the hairs and triggers the trap, which snaps together tightly.

A fly attracted by the nectar lands on the trap.

The bristles stop the fly from wriggling out of the trap.

The trap is the hinged flaps at the tip of the leaf.

Glands in the trap release fluids that turn the fly into liquid, ready to be digested.

Growing plant

The seed sprouts, or germinates, in the boggy soil. The plant grows slowly, producing several long leaves. At the tip of each leaf is a trap—a pair of hinged flaps fringed with stiff, comb-like bristles. The flaps produce sweet nectar that attract insects, such as this fly.

Venus flytraps can live for more than 20 years in the wild.

See also
Read about plants that have a friendlier relationship with insects: the orchid (58–59) and the rafflesia (66–67).

Creating seeds

Pollinated flowers produce round, black seed capsules. The tiny seeds mature four to six weeks after pollination. Venus flytraps also reproduce by sending out underground stems called rhizomes. These separate and become new plants.

Making flowers

It may take three to four years for the plant to flower. The flowers grow on a long stem high above the traps. This keeps pollinating insects attracted by the flowers' scent from accidentally getting caught.

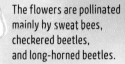

The flowers are pollinated mainly by sweat bees, checkered beetles, and long-horned beetles.

Sensitive plant
The mimosa, also known as "the sensitive plant," is another type of plant with quick reactions. Its leaves soon droop if it is touched. This makes the plant look sickly and persuades browsing animals to look elsewhere for a meal.

Venus flytrap

The extraordinary Venus flytrap is a carnivorous plant, which means it catches and "eats" unsuspecting insects and spiders that make the mistake of landing on its snapping traps. By devouring its prey in this way, it gets most of the nutrients it needs, since the poor, boggy soil that it grows in provides little nourishment.

Pitcher plant
This plant has a trap shaped like a jug. Insects tempted by nectar at the rim of the trap slip on its waxy surface and tumble inside. They drown in liquid at the bottom and are then eaten.

Strangler fig

Unlike rafflesia, the strangler fig kills its host plant. The seed germinates in a branch crevice high up in a tree. It then grows roots down to the ground, "strangling" the host tree, which withers and dies.

Tarantula hawk wasp

This wasp paralyzes a spider with its sting before laying an egg on the spider's abdomen. The wasp larva burrows into the spider and feeds, avoiding vital organs to keep the spider alive for as long as possible.

Growing bud

The threads spread inside the vine for up to 18 months. At flowering time, a small rafflesia bud bursts through the bark of the vine's woody stem. It may take up to nine months for the bud to fully develop, by which time it resembles a large cabbage.

Rafflesia

Also known as the corpse lily, rafflesia is the world's largest single flower. You can usually smell it before you see it—it reeks like decaying flesh! This amazing plant lives hidden inside forest vines as a parasite. Only when rafflesia flowers can you actually see it.

Living off the vine

A rafflesia seed lodges in the roots or stem of a vine. It germinates and sends out tiny threads to absorb water and nutrients. The vine may be weakened, but it won't die.

Leaves of the host vine

Big bloom

The enormous rafflesia flower wafts out its foul fragrance of decaying meat. It is pollinated by carrion flies, which feed on rotting flesh. They are tricked into visiting the flower by the smell.

The flower can be over 3 ft (1 m) wide.

Fleshy fruit

After a few days, the huge flower withers and collapses into a slimy black mass. The fruit produced by the flower has a woody skin and smooth, cream-colored flesh containing thousands of tiny seeds.

Spreading the seeds

Tree shrews and other animals come to eat the fruit, scooping out the flesh with their paws. They spread the rafflesia seeds through the forest in their droppings, or on their fur and paws.

See also
Many plants are pollinated by insects—read about the coconut palm (56–57) and the Venus flytrap (64–65).

Animals

The life cycles of animals are as varied as the animals themselves. Some manage to fertilize one another by scattering their sperm and eggs in open water and leaving them to chance. Others meet and mate to fertilize. And many animals care for their babies so they have the best possible start in life.

Octopus

Octopuses are brainy creatures—they are among the most intelligent of all animals. The giant Pacific octopus can learn to open a jar or find its way through a maze for food. However, they are not very sociable—males and females live alone and hunt a variety of sea creatures, including smaller octopuses.

Chemical attraction

To attract a male, the female releases a chemical. As the male swims toward her, his skin color darkens. The male uses one of his eight arms for mating. About one month later, the male dies.

Strands of eggs

After mating, the female lays up to 100,000 eggs, hanging them in her den like strings of pearls. She protects and cleans the eggs until, seven months later, they hatch. And then she dies.

Growing up

Young octopuses continue to grow until they mate, at three to five years old. A fully grown female giant Pacific octopus is strong enough to move up to 700 lb (320 kg) using all eight arms. This is about the weight of a small pig.

Octopuses feed on crabs and other sea creatures.

See also
Explore other life in the watery world of coral (72–73).

Hatching out

After the eggs hatch, baby octopuses float up to the surface of the water. Here, they become part of the plankton (tiny living organisms that float in water). They live there for a few months before swimming to the bottom of the ocean.

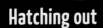

Mimic octopus This is the only sea creature that can copy, or mimic, different kinds of animals, including poisonous ones like sea snakes. It does this by changing its color, shape, and texture.

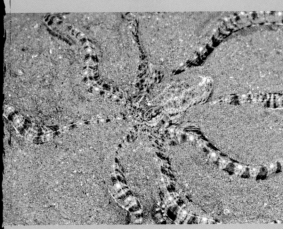

Coconut octopus Also called the veined octopus, this animal can walk on two of its arms, using the other six to carry a clam or coconut shell, which it uses as a mobile home.

Argonaut octopus Instead of laying her eggs in a den or cave, this female secretes, or produces, a shell-like egg case to protect her eggs and then lives in it.

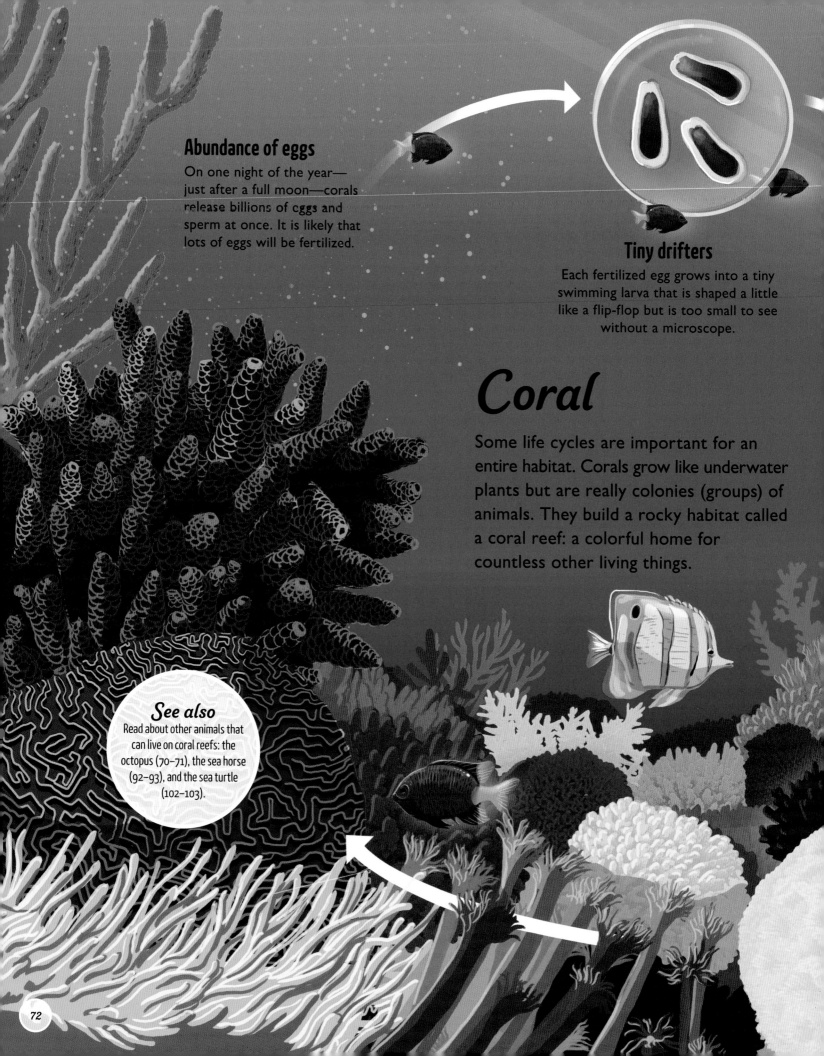

Abundance of eggs

On one night of the year—just after a full moon—corals release billions of eggs and sperm at once. It is likely that lots of eggs will be fertilized.

Tiny drifters

Each fertilized egg grows into a tiny swimming larva that is shaped a little like a flip-flop but is too small to see without a microscope.

Coral

Some life cycles are important for an entire habitat. Corals grow like underwater plants but are really colonies (groups) of animals. They build a rocky habitat called a coral reef: a colorful home for countless other living things.

See also

Read about other animals that can live on coral reefs: the octopus (70–71), the sea horse (92–93), and the sea turtle (102–103).

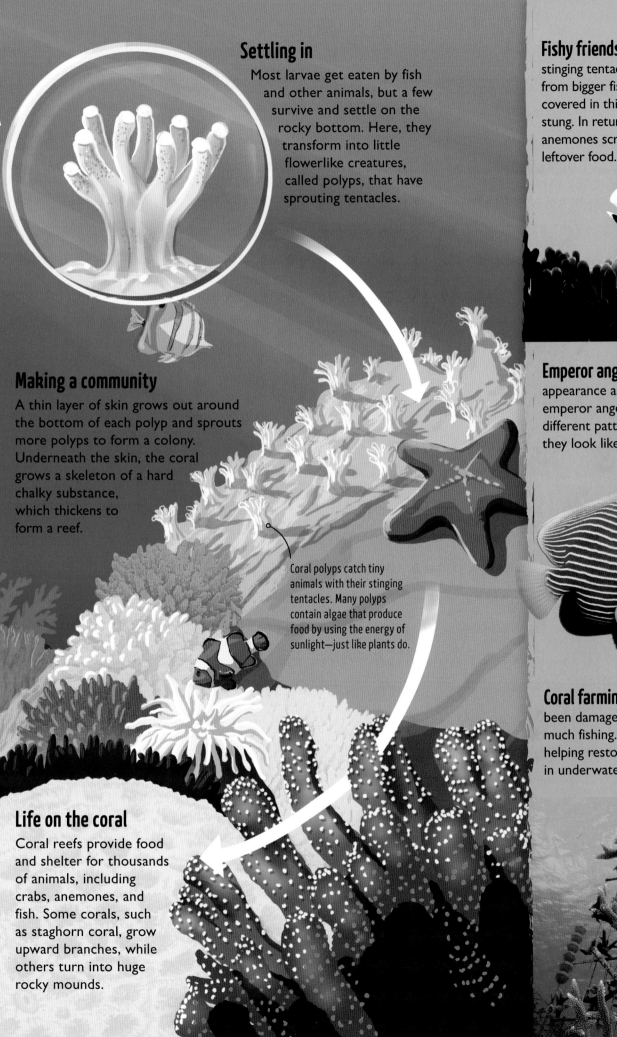

Settling in

Most larvae get eaten by fish and other animals, but a few survive and settle on the rocky bottom. Here, they transform into little flowerlike creatures, called polyps, that have sprouting tentacles.

Making a community

A thin layer of skin grows out around the bottom of each polyp and sprouts more polyps to form a colony. Underneath the skin, the coral grows a skeleton of a hard chalky substance, which thickens to form a reef.

Coral polyps catch tiny animals with their stinging tentacles. Many polyps contain algae that produce food by using the energy of sunlight—just like plants do.

Life on the coral

Coral reefs provide food and shelter for thousands of animals, including crabs, anemones, and fish. Some corals, such as staghorn coral, grow upward branches, while others turn into huge rocky mounds.

Fishy friends

Sea anemones use their stinging tentacles to protect clown fish from bigger fish. The clown fish are covered in thick slime so they don't get stung. In return, the clown fish gives sea anemones scraps of leftover food.

Emperor angelfish

Some fish change appearance as they grow. A young emperor angelfish has a completely different pattern than an adult, so they look like different types of fish.

Coral farming

Sadly, many reefs have been damaged by pollution and too much fishing. Some scientists are helping restore them by growing corals in underwater nurseries.

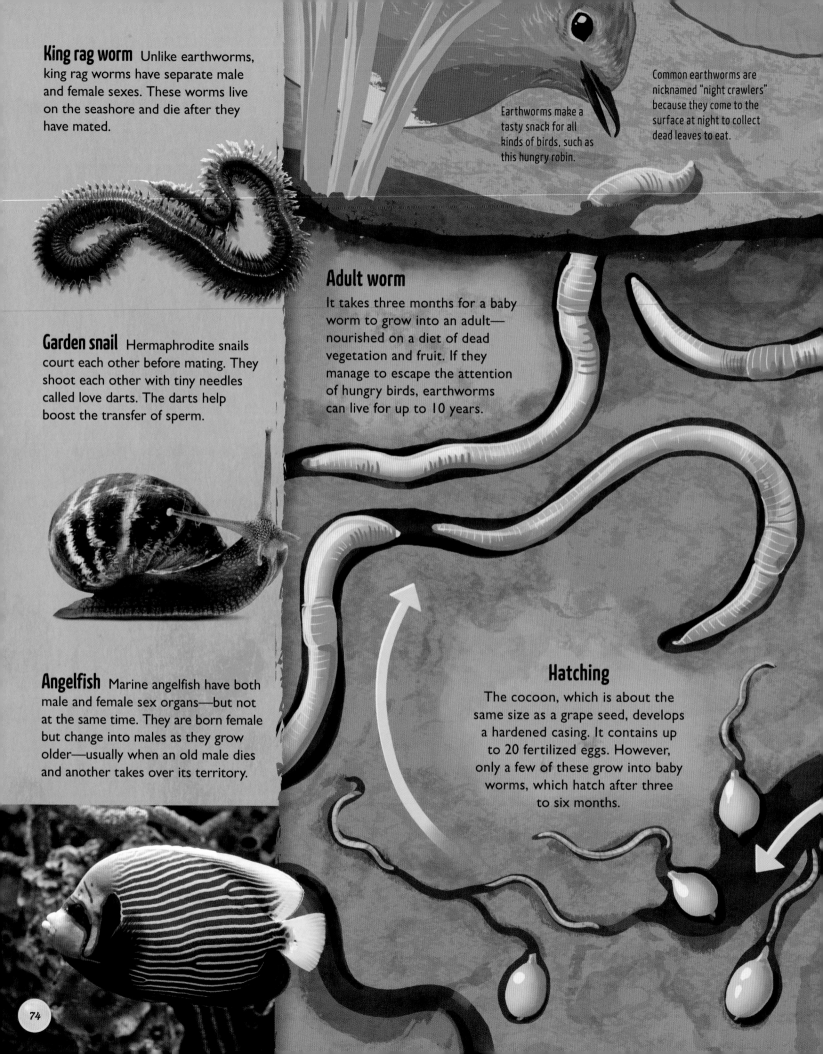

King rag worm Unlike earthworms, king rag worms have separate male and female sexes. These worms live on the seashore and die after they have mated.

Earthworms make a tasty snack for all kinds of birds, such as this hungry robin.

Common earthworms are nicknamed "night crawlers" because they come to the surface at night to collect dead leaves to eat.

Garden snail Hermaphrodite snails court each other before mating. They shoot each other with tiny needles called love darts. The darts help boost the transfer of sperm.

Adult worm

It takes three months for a baby worm to grow into an adult— nourished on a diet of dead vegetation and fruit. If they manage to escape the attention of hungry birds, earthworms can live for up to 10 years.

Angelfish Marine angelfish have both male and female sex organs—but not at the same time. They are born female but change into males as they grow older—usually when an old male dies and another takes over its territory.

Hatching

The cocoon, which is about the same size as a grape seed, develops a hardened casing. It contains up to 20 fertilized eggs. However, only a few of these grow into baby worms, which hatch after three to six months.

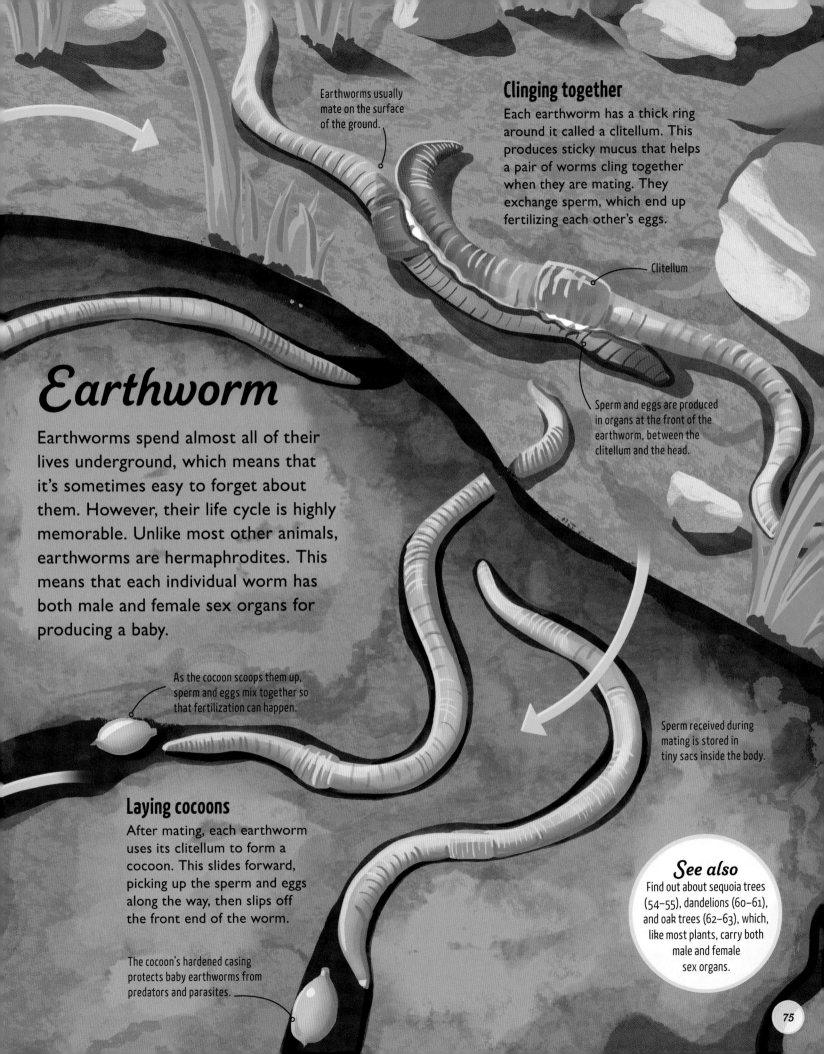

Earthworms usually mate on the surface of the ground.

Clinging together

Each earthworm has a thick ring around it called a clitellum. This produces sticky mucus that helps a pair of worms cling together when they are mating. They exchange sperm, which end up fertilizing each other's eggs.

Clitellum

Sperm and eggs are produced in organs at the front of the earthworm, between the clitellum and the head.

Earthworm

Earthworms spend almost all of their lives underground, which means that it's sometimes easy to forget about them. However, their life cycle is highly memorable. Unlike most other animals, earthworms are hermaphrodites. This means that each individual worm has both male and female sex organs for producing a baby.

As the cocoon scoops them up, sperm and eggs mix together so that fertilization can happen.

Sperm received during mating is stored in tiny sacs inside the body.

Laying cocoons

After mating, each earthworm uses its clitellum to form a cocoon. This slides forward, picking up the sperm and eggs along the way, then slips off the front end of the worm.

The cocoon's hardened casing protects baby earthworms from predators and parasites.

See also
Find out about sequoia trees (54–55), dandelions (60–61), and oak trees (62–63), which, like most plants, carry both male and female sex organs.

Spider

Many spiders produce silk and make sticky webs to trap prey. The yellow-and-black garden spider spins a web like a bicycle wheel to catch flying insects, including flies, grasshoppers, and wasps. The females are the main web builders, weaving a new web each day.

Making a web

The female spider builds the frame of her web by attaching silk threads to surfaces such as plant stems. Then she lays a spiral of dry silk to hold the threads in place and finally adds a spiral of sticky silk.

Spiders use silk produced by organs called spinnerets at the end of their abdomens.

Silk threads radiate out from the center like the spokes of a bicycle wheel.

The spider stays in the middle, waiting for insects to be caught.

A spiral of sticky silk traps insects that land on the web.

Zigzag bands may help birds see the web so that they don't blunder into it.

Good vibrations

When a male spider arrives to court the female, he plucks the silk strands of her web to make it vibrate. If she likes the pattern of the vibrations, she mates with him. The male dies during mating, and the female sometimes eats his body afterward.

The male sometimes waves his legs around and dances to impress the female.

Gift wrapped

The male nursery-web spider gives a present of food, wrapped in silk, to the female he hopes to mate with. A male that turns up empty-handed is more likely to be eaten by the female.

Daddy longlegs

The female daddy longlegs spider bundles up her eggs with a few strands of silk. She carries the eggs around in her jaws until they hatch. During this time, she is unable to eat.

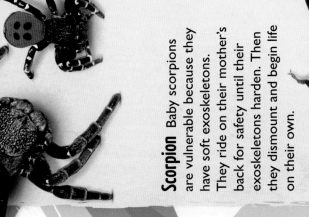

Ladybird spider In many spider species, the males are much smaller than the females, but ladybird spiders have different colors too. The male has a bright red, spotted body, while the female is jet black.

Scorpion Baby scorpions are vulnerable because they have soft exoskeletons. They ride on their mother's back for safety until their exoskeletons harden. Then they dismount and begin life on their own.

Wrapped in silk

The female lays her eggs on a mat of silk and covers them with more threads. Then she molds the silky mass into a ball-shaped egg sac and attaches it to a nearby surface.

The female watches over her eggs for as long as she can. She will die when it gets colder.

See also
Read about the king cobra (104–105), who is a venomous mom too—and also guards her eggs.

Tiny spiderlings

Between 300 and 1,400 baby spiders (spiderlings) hatch from the eggs in the sac. In cooler climates, spiderlings that hatch in fall stay in the sac until spring so they don't freeze to death.

Roaming far away

Some spiderlings remain nearby. Others spin a strand of silk that gets caught by the breeze and carries them to new places, where there is hopefully less competition for food and mates. This is called ballooning.

Ant

Families don't get much bigger than a colony of ants. Hundreds of them share a single mom: an egg-laying queen. Most kinds of ants live in nests, but army ants from South American rain forests move from place to place as they hunt prey.

Queen

The queen ant's body swells to ay tens of thousands of eggs per week. During this time, her workers swarm around her in a huge protective bundle.

When a swarm is settled in one place, it is called a bivouac.

On the move

As the larvae grow, the entire ant colony moves to a different place. The ants march in aggressive columns along trails that they mark with their scent, attacking small animals in their path.

Ants are virtually blind, so they rely on touch and smell to get around.

Ants swarm over insects and other prey, kill them with their stings, and pull them apart to provide meat for the colony.

Egg to larva

Each egg grows into the next stage—a wriggling, wormlike larva, which is looked after by the workers. Ants get restless as more larvae build up.

Larva to pupa

Each larva turns into a pupa. This is the stage when ants develop into adults by a complete change in body shape. Larvae and pupae cannot walk, so adult ants must carry them.

This adult worker ant is carrying a pupa.

Becoming ants

The pupae develop into different kinds of adult ants—female soldiers and workers and male drones. Each type has its own job to do.

Drone

The queen also produces unfertilized eggs that develop into sons called drones. Unlike the other ants, drones have wings so they can fly to other colonies and mate with other queens.

Worker

Other adults are workers. They kill small animals to provide food for the colony. They carry larvae or pupae when the colony is on the move. Like soldier ants, they develop from fertilized eggs.

Soldier

Adults with the biggest jaws are called soldiers. They are daughters of the queen and develop from fertilized eggs. Soldier ants are the most aggressive and will bite to help defend the colony.

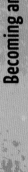

See also

Read about the breeding habits of other adult female insects, such as butterflies (80–81) and dragonflies (82–83).

Potter wasp Other kinds of wasps build their nests from mud, which dries to form a tough container, just like a clay pot.

Paper wasp Many wasps build nests from chewed wood and plant fibers with their saliva. The mixture then hardens in the sun.

Honeybee Unlike army ants, honeybees live in a fixed nest called a hive. They feed on pollen and nectar instead of meat.

Butterfly

A fluttering adult butterfly looks nothing like the crawling caterpillar it once was when it was young. That's because it has undergone a dramatic life change called complete metamorphosis. Like other insects that go through this transformation, the monarch butterfly, shown here, has four life stages: egg, larva, pupa, and adult.

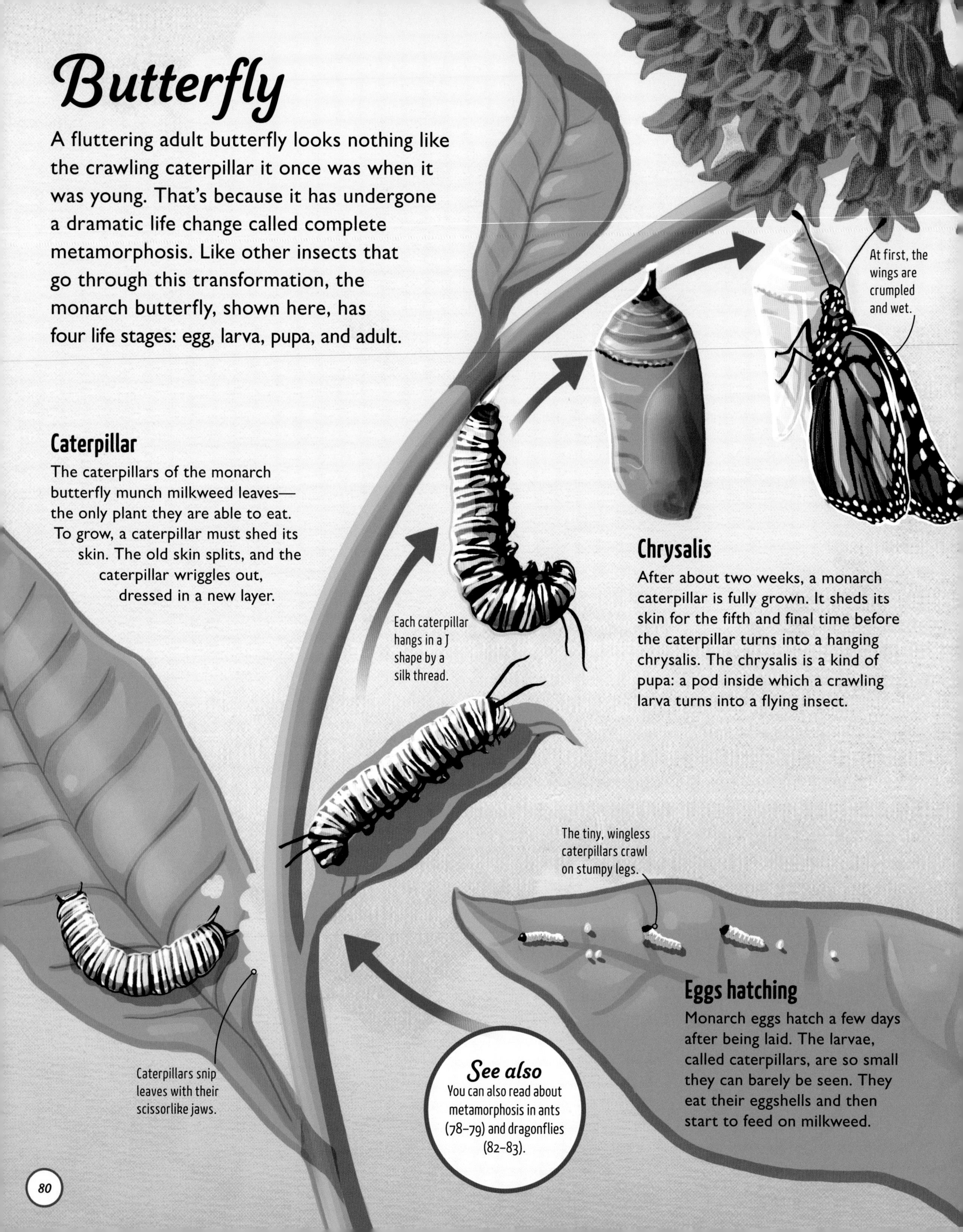

Caterpillar

The caterpillars of the monarch butterfly munch milkweed leaves—the only plant they are able to eat. To grow, a caterpillar must shed its skin. The old skin splits, and the caterpillar wriggles out, dressed in a new layer.

At first, the wings are crumpled and wet.

Each caterpillar hangs in a J shape by a silk thread.

Chrysalis

After about two weeks, a monarch caterpillar is fully grown. It sheds its skin for the fifth and final time before the caterpillar turns into a hanging chrysalis. The chrysalis is a kind of pupa: a pod inside which a crawling larva turns into a flying insect.

The tiny, wingless caterpillars crawl on stumpy legs.

Caterpillars snip leaves with their scissorlike jaws.

See also
You can also read about metamorphosis in ants (78–79) and dragonflies (82–83).

Eggs hatching

Monarch eggs hatch a few days after being laid. The larvae, called caterpillars, are so small they can barely be seen. They eat their eggshells and then start to feed on milkweed.

Soon, the wings unfold and dry out.

Mass migration In fall, millions of monarch butterflies travel south from Canada and the United States to spend winter in Mexico. There, they huddle together in trees to stay warm. In spring, they head north again.

Butterfly

In another 8–14 days, the chrysalis splits and a butterfly emerges. After about an hour, it is ready to fly. Instead of chomping leaves like it did as a caterpillar, the butterfly now sips flower nectar through a long tube called a proboscis.

A monarch butterfly can breed between three to eight days after emerging from the chrysalis.

Some monarch butterflies migrate over 3,000 miles (5,000 km) from Canada to Mexico.

Moth silk cocoon Like butterflies, moths also go through complete metamorphosis, but many don't form a hard chrysalis. Instead, they spin a silk covering around the pupa called a cocoon. The silk can be used to make clothing.

Laying eggs

Females begin to lay eggs right after mating. The eggs, which are the size of pinheads, are laid singly and glued to milkweed leaves. A female monarch may lay 300–500 eggs over her lifetime.

Drying out

The dragonfly waits for its legs and body to harden and its wings to dry out in the sun. Then it begins hunting for food, such as mosquitoes, flies, bees, and butterflies—and it starts searching for a mate.

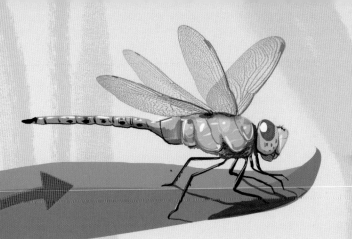

The emerging adult hauls out its soft new body and carefully uncurls its abdomen.

Emerging dragonfly

The nymph leaves the water for good, ready for the last molt of its life. It puffs up its exoskeleton, causing it to split open. The dragonfly wriggles out, ready for life as an adult.

Dragonfly

Fast-flying dragonflies, like the green darner shown here, dart through the air beside lakes, ponds, and streams. Young dragonflies, called nymphs, look like adults but have no wings. The nymphs change into adults through shedding, or molting, their exoskeletons (outer skeletons). This is called incomplete metamorphosis.

The nymph emerges from its watery world, often by crawling up a plant stem.

Powerful wings allow dragonflies to fly at 30 mph (50 kph).

Molting

Instead of stretchy skin, the nymph has a hard covering called an exoskeleton. It must shed, or molt, its exoskeleton regularly so that it can grow. The stage between each molt is called an instar.

See also
Compare this life cycle with that of the praying mantis (84–85), which also goes through incomplete metamorphosis.

The dragonfly's adult wings start to develop, but for now they remain tucked inside wing pads.

Mating

When mating, the male grasps the female's head using claspers at the end of his abdomen (the long taillike part). She curls her abdomen underneath him so that he can fertilize her eggs.

Dragonflies may mate on a perch, or even in midair while still flying.

Laying eggs

The female green darner inserts her eggs into tiny slits that she makes in the stems of water plants. Often the male will hold her while she is laying eggs.

Hatching

The larva that hatches from the egg is called a nymph. Breathing through gills in its rectum (bottom), a dragonfly nymph lives underwater for months or even years, depending on the species.

The nymph is a fierce hunter of small fish, tadpoles, and insect larvae.

Prehistoric ancestors
Fossils show that dragonflies evolved around 300 million years ago. Some ancient dragonflies were scarily big, with wingspans of up to 2 ft (60 cm).

Mosquito
Like dragonflies, mosquitoes live underwater when they're larvae. Unlike dragonflies, however, they go through complete metamorphosis—the larvae turn into floating pupae before becoming winged adults.

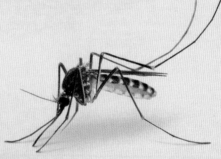

Mayfly
Mayflies have a larval stage in water, too. Once out in the air, they often live for no more than a day as adults. The adults don't feed—they spend their brief time mating, and then they die.

Ready to breed

When a female European mantis is ready to breed, she releases chemicals called pheromones into the air to attract a male.

Praying mantis

Mantises are deadly predators, snatching prey with their spine-clad legs and shredding it with their jaws. These insects can also be a danger to each other. Many female praying mantises, including this European mantis, eat the male after mating. The nutrients from the male's body help the female produce more eggs.

Easy does it

A male arrives and cautiously approaches the female. He positions himself behind her, to stop her from attacking him before they mate.

Devouring dad

After, or even during mating, the female sometimes decides to eat her male partner. She first bites off his head and then devours the rest of his body.

Hold tight!

The male leaps onto the female's back. After stroking her with his antennae to calm her down, the pair mate.

Scary display

When threatened, many mantis species stand tall, spread their forelegs, and fan out their wings to make themselves look larger and more fearsome. This is enough to make some predators back off.

No boys allowed

Brunner's stick mantis is an all-female species, so there are no males to be eaten! The young are tiny clones (copies) of their mother. This kind of breeding is called parthenogenesis.

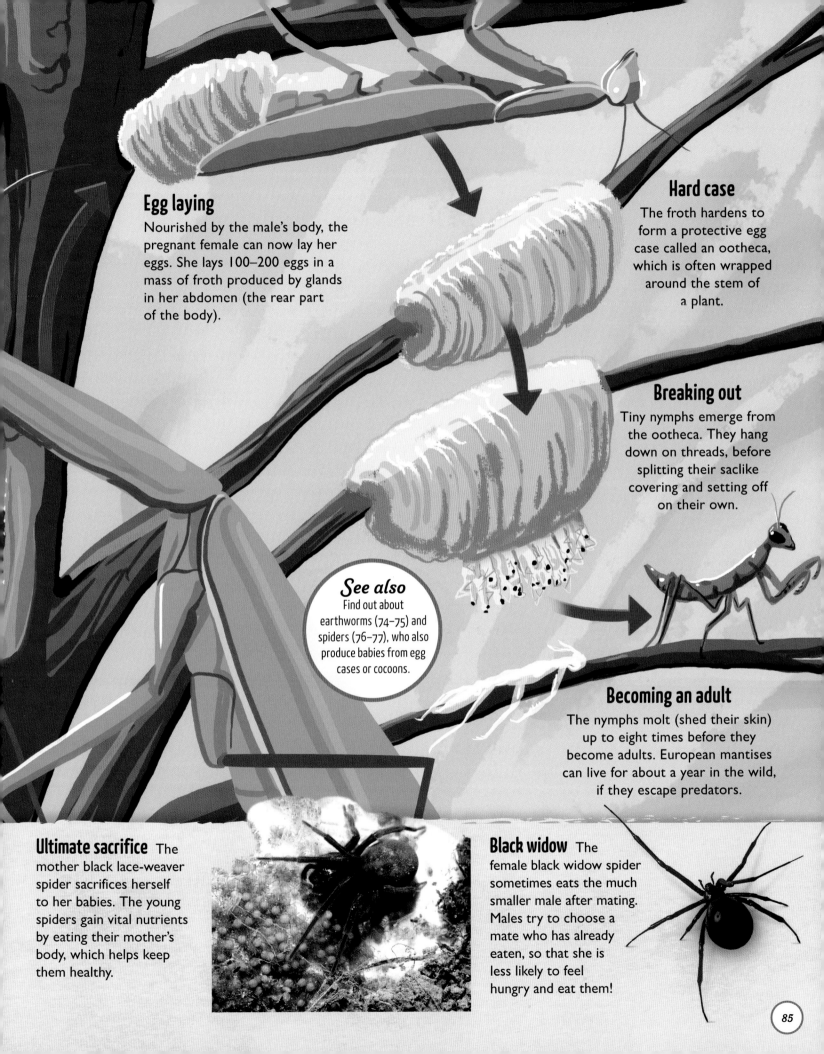

Egg laying

Nourished by the male's body, the pregnant female can now lay her eggs. She lays 100–200 eggs in a mass of froth produced by glands in her abdomen (the rear part of the body).

Hard case

The froth hardens to form a protective egg case called an ootheca, which is often wrapped around the stem of a plant.

Breaking out

Tiny nymphs emerge from the ootheca. They hang down on threads, before splitting their saclike covering and setting off on their own.

See also

Find out about earthworms (74–75) and spiders (76–77), who also produce babies from egg cases or cocoons.

Becoming an adult

The nymphs molt (shed their skin) up to eight times before they become adults. European mantises can live for about a year in the wild, if they escape predators.

Ultimate sacrifice

The mother black lace-weaver spider sacrifices herself to her babies. The young spiders gain vital nutrients by eating their mother's body, which helps keep them healthy.

Black widow

The female black widow spider sometimes eats the much smaller male after mating. Males try to choose a mate who has already eaten, so that she is less likely to feel hungry and eat them!

Life *in* water

Water covers nearly three-quarters of our planet's surface, and the first life evolved in the oceans. So it's no surprise that so many living things make water their home. Animals with gills spend their entire lives submerged, but others that breathe air must occasionally come to the surface to survive.

Freshwater

Rivers

Freshwater falling as rain on land gathers in channels and ultimately flows downhill to the ocean. Life thrives at every stage, from tumbling streams and waterfalls to wide, slow rivers.

Manatees make their home in rivers.

Diving beetles can survive in small ponds.

Coral reef

Tiny anemone-like animals called coral polyps grow in colonies that produce rocky skeletons called reefs. Coral reefs grow around warm coastlines and are home to more kinds of animals than any other ocean habitat.

Mangrove swamp

Few land plants can survive in salty ocean water, but mangrove trees are an exception. They grow rooted in mud along tropical shorelines, providing a forest habitat for animals that live between the land and the sea.

Bogs and marshes

Some kinds of plants can take root in pools of water, while others float on the surface, creating dense vegetation. These bogs and marshes provide good cover for predators and prey alike.

Ponds and lakes

Some animals can survive in ponds or tiny pools. These can dry up in times of drought. Other creatures live in deep lakes so big you cannot see the other side.

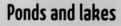

Caimans hunt for fish and the occasional water bird on the marshy banks of the Amazon River in South America.

Huge pipe sponges sprout among the corals of a reef.

Air-breathing seals rely on holes in the ice to survive.

Polar seas

At the Earth's poles, the sun's rays are too feeble to generate much warmth, meaning oceans are so cold that ice forms on the surface. Yet fish, seals, and whales thrive in the fertile water underneath, which is rich with sea creatures to feed on.

Saltwater

Deep sea

The deep sea is the Earth's biggest habitat. Most of it is cold and black because sunlight cannot reach it, but even here there is life.

Open ocean

Microscopic algae float at the surface of the ocean and make a tasty meal for fish, whales, and other sea creatures. In open waters, there is nowhere to hide—and animals must blend in or have the speed to escape danger or catch prey.

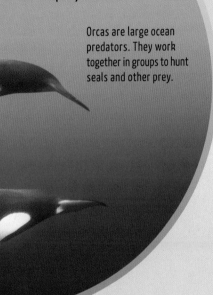

Orcas are large ocean predators. They work together in groups to hunt seals and other prey.

A whipnose angler lives deep down underwater and lures prey using an illuminated fishing line.

Seashore

Some coastal animals prefer shorelines that are hard and rocky. Others need softer shores covered in mud or sand. But all animals of the seashore must cope with the regular coming and going of the ocean's tides.

Seabird

Water collecting between rocks at the seashore creates tide pool habitats for animals such as anemones and crabs.

Starfish

Crab

Side by side

Lemon sharks mate in shallow waters. Swimming alongside the female, the male grabs the female's pectoral fin in his jaws to keep her close to him, ready for mating.

Breeding bunch

Male and female lemon sharks make long migrations from the waters where they feed to special breeding sites. They gather together in large numbers.

Shark

Like most sharks, the female lemon shark gives birth to her young, who can swim as soon as they're born. The baby sharks, called pups, are born near special "nursery" areas, such as coastal mangrove forests. Here, there is plenty of shelter and food to give youngsters the best chance of survival.

To the nursery

After 10 to 12 months, it is time to give birth. The female swims to the edge of the mangroves. This is the "nursery," where her pups will spend their first years.

Tailfirst

The mother can have more than 10 pups per litter. The pup emerges from its mother tailfirst, still attached by its umbilical cord. As the pup swims away, the umbilical cord breaks.

Shark eggs Some sharks are egg layers. The eggs are protected by leathery cases with tendrils that attach to coral, seaweed, or the seafloor. The mother leaves the eggs to hatch on their own.

Sand tiger shark The first pup to develop inside the mother sand tiger shark eats its unborn brothers and sisters. The little cannibal then continues to feed on the eggs that are left.

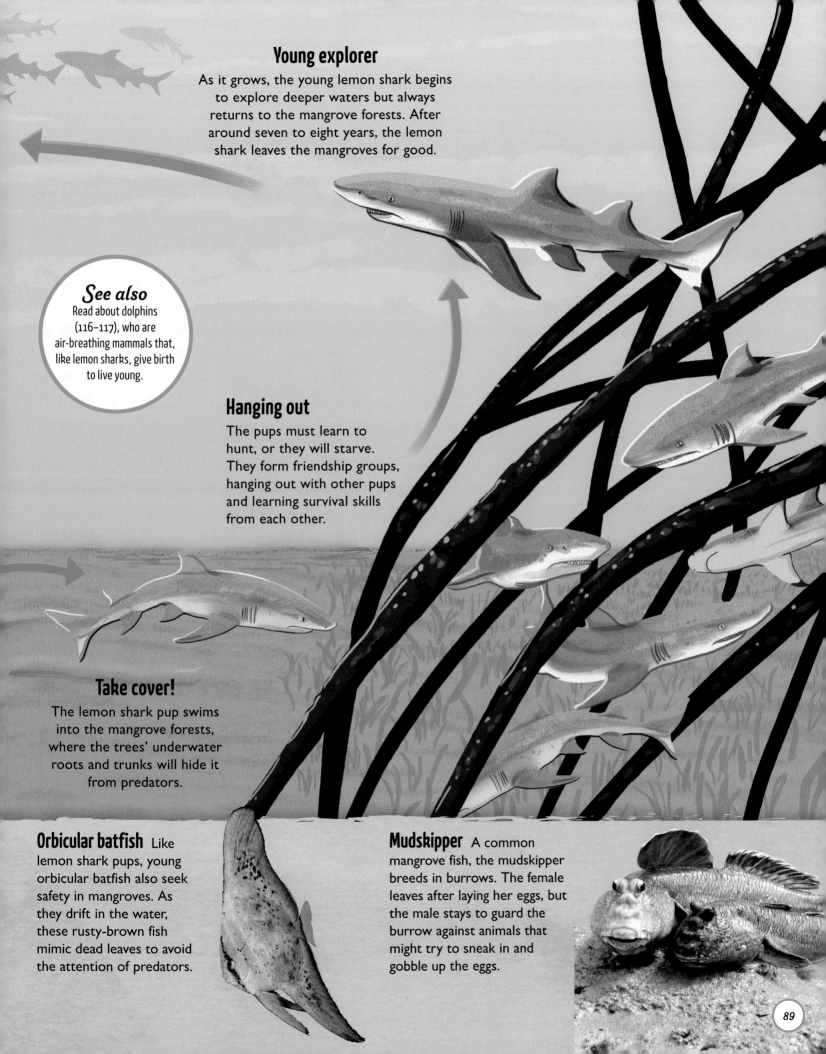

Young explorer

As it grows, the young lemon shark begins to explore deeper waters but always returns to the mangrove forests. After around seven to eight years, the lemon shark leaves the mangroves for good.

See also
Read about dolphins (116–117), who are air-breathing mammals that, like lemon sharks, give birth to live young.

Hanging out

The pups must learn to hunt, or they will starve. They form friendship groups, hanging out with other pups and learning survival skills from each other.

Take cover!

The lemon shark pup swims into the mangrove forests, where the trees' underwater roots and trunks will hide it from predators.

Orbicular batfish Like lemon shark pups, young orbicular batfish also seek safety in mangroves. As they drift in the water, these rusty-brown fish mimic dead leaves to avoid the attention of predators.

Mudskipper A common mangrove fish, the mudskipper breeds in burrows. The female leaves after laying her eggs, but the male stays to guard the burrow against animals that might try to sneak in and gobble up the eggs.

Young fish

After a few weeks, the baby salmon, called fry, are already good swimmers. They leave the stream where they were born and swim into lakes to find food. They mostly eat insects, and some plankton.

Changing color

By the time they are two years old, the young salmon, called smolt, have changed color and are now silver with red tails. They swim downriver into an estuary, where they adapt to salty water before swimming out to sea.

Hatching out

Newly hatched salmon are called alevin. They are tiny—just 1 inch (2.5 cm) long. They have a large yolk sac, which they feed on.

Eggs

The female makes a nest in the gravel at the bottom of a shallow stream and lays 50–200 eggs. The male dies after he fertilizes the eggs, and the female dies soon after. The eggs remain in the nest for 32–42 days.

Swimming upriver

To breed, or spawn, salmon swim up the same river they once swam down as young fish. They jump rapids and avoid hungry bears. Those that survive the "salmon run" are exhausted by the effort.

To the sea

The smolt mature into adult salmon once they reach the ocean. They spend up to four years at sea, feeding on tiny animals called zooplankton. Sockeye salmon are found at depths of 50–108 ft (15–33 m) in the Pacific Ocean.

See also

Find out about the octopus (70–71), who also dies after breeding.

Salmon

Sockeye salmon go through many changes in their lives. They move from one habitat to another—from freshwater to salty water, and then back to fresh. They switch from eating insects to plankton. And they change color—from clear to light green, through to silver, then blue, and finally red.

Grizzly bear These fearsome bears love to feed on salmon. As the salmon swim upriver to spawn, the bears wade out into the rapids to fish for them.

Freshwater eel The journey, or migration, that salmon make to breed, from sea to river, is called anadromous. Freshwater eels follow the opposite pattern, swimming from river to sea. This migration is called catadromous.

Century plant Salmon reproduce just once in their lives. This behavior is also found in plants, such as the century plant, which flowers once and then dies.

Sea horse

Sea horses are very unusual fish. The spotted sea horse has armor instead of scales. It has eyes that move independently, fins so tiny that it has trouble swimming, and a tail that can grab objects and other sea horses. Strangest of all, it is the father who protects the eggs in his pouch, feeds them with nutrients, and even gives birth.

Courtship

When a female sea horse is ready to mate, she moves closer to the male and starts a courtship dance, nodding her head toward him. The male may inflate his pouch in response.

Courting sea horses often swim holding each other's tails.

The sea horses can dance together for hours, even days.

After the female transfers her eggs, she looks thinner and the male fatter.

Pregnant male

The male's pouch is similar in some ways to the uterus, or womb, of a female mammal. The male produces nutrients, including some from seawater, that seep into the pouch and keep the eggs healthy.

Egg transfer

The courtship dance ends with the female transferring her eggs to the male. The female inserts a tube into the male's pouch and passes her eggs to him. The eggs are then fertilized in the male's pouch.

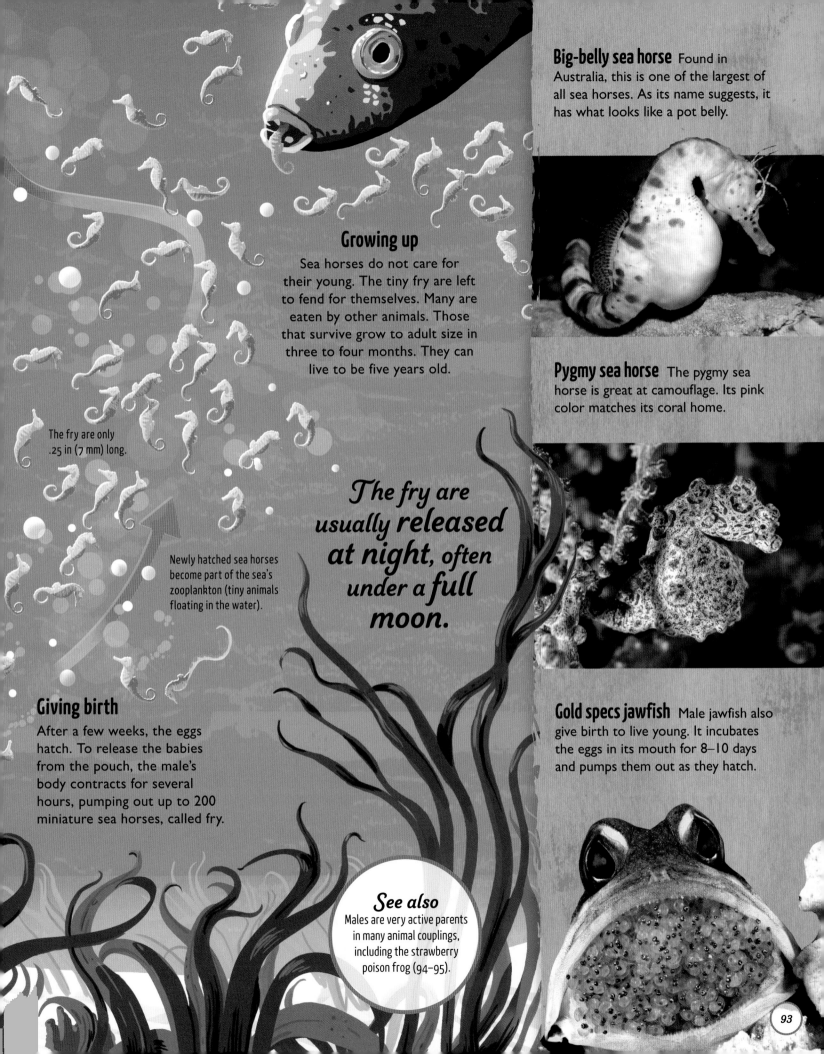

Growing up

Sea horses do not care for their young. The tiny fry are left to fend for themselves. Many are eaten by other animals. Those that survive grow to adult size in three to four months. They can live to be five years old.

The fry are only .25 in (7 mm) long.

Newly hatched sea horses become part of the sea's zooplankton (tiny animals floating in the water).

The fry are usually released at night, often under a full moon.

Giving birth

After a few weeks, the eggs hatch. To release the babies from the pouch, the male's body contracts for several hours, pumping out up to 200 miniature sea horses, called fry.

Big-belly sea horse
Found in Australia, this is one of the largest of all sea horses. As its name suggests, it has what looks like a pot belly.

Pygmy sea horse
The pygmy sea horse is great at camouflage. Its pink color matches its coral home.

Gold specs jawfish
Male jawfish also give birth to live young. It incubates the eggs in its mouth for 8–10 days and pumps them out as they hatch.

See also
Males are very active parents in many animal couplings, including the strawberry poison frog (94–95).

93

Frog

Many frogs are surprisingly active parents. They spend a lot of time keeping their eggs moist and their tadpoles wet. Like most amphibians, frogs require water to complete their life cycle. This can be a challenge even in the tropical rain forests of Central America, the home of the strawberry poison frog.

The frog's colors warn predators that its skin contains deadly chemicals.

Guarding the eggs

The male guards the eggs, keeping them clean and moist with urine until they hatch into tadpoles.

Mating

A male attracts a female with his calls and may crawl onto her back before releasing sperm on a leaf. The female then lays her eggs so they can be fertilized by the sperm.

Carrying tadpoles

The female returns when the eggs begin to hatch. She sits on them and waits for a tadpole to wriggle onto her back. Then she crawls backward into a pool of water on the bromeliad plant and waits for the tadpole to swim away.

Growing limbs

A young tadpole has fishlike gills and a ong tail for swimming. It feeds on the mother's unfertilized eggs, and after a few weeks it develops limbs. This process is called metamorphosis.

Froglet

The tadpole soon loses its gills and develops lungs so it can breathe air. It is now called a froglet, and it begins to eat small insects. It remains near the pool until it loses its tail.

Frogs can lay thousands of eggs at a time.

Axolotl Unlike other amphibians, this large salamander has external gills and a fishlike tail. It does not undergo a full metamorphosis and lives its whole life in water.

Midwife toad This male frog carries a string of eggs on his back, with the egg string wrapped around his ankles. He walks into shallow water when they are ready to hatch.

Adult life

The frog is now fully grown. It lives among layers of leaves, making it hard to spot in the rain forest. The best way to find one is to listen for the calls of the males guarding their territory.

Darwin's frog Just before his tadpoles hatch, the father gathers them into his throat sac. He holds them until they have hatched and the froglets can hop out on their own.

See also
Read about how different kinds of insects go through metamorphosis (78–85).

Dinosaurs *through* time

Dinosaurs were an incredibly successful and varied group of animals. They ruled the Earth during the Mesozoic era, from about 252 to 66 million years ago, and spread to all continents. They ranged in size from tiny two-legged meat eaters to long-necked giants that would dwarf any land animal alive today.

Stegosaurus's plates may have been used for display.

Eoraptor

The Triassic period

This period opened on a barren landscape in the wake of the Permian-Triassic extinction, which had wiped out more than 90 percent of life on Earth. With little competition, dinosaurs would soon dominate.

The first dinosaurs

Herrerasaurus and Eoraptor are among the earliest dinosaurs we know about. Both walked on two legs and were discovered in Argentina. Around the same time, the earliest mammals evolved.

Triassic extinction

At the end of the Triassic period, an extinction event eliminated many species, including other reptiles. New dinosaurs emerged in their place.

Jurassic giants

As the continents split apart, the climate became wetter, and lush rain forests sprang up. Dinosaurs flourished and large, powerful species emerged, such as Stegosaurus, Allosaurus, and Brachiosaurus.

Dinosauromorphs

From the ashes of extinction, a strange group of reptiles emerged. Dinosauromorphs were small, lightly built animals that could walk on both two and four legs. They would evolve into the first dinosaurs.

Getting bigger

Although most were quite small, larger dinosaurs such as Plateosaurus began to emerge. It was around 26 ft (8 m) long.

Plateosaurus

252 mya

249 mya

200 mya

201 mya

235 mya

210 mya

mya = million years ago

145
mya

66.25
mya

66
mya

Today

Volcanic eruptions

For 250,000 years, gigantic volcanoes erupted in India, spewing ash and lava. However, this alone was not enough to cause the extinction of the dinosaurs.

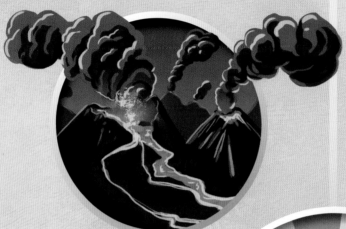

Modern dinosaurs

All the birds alive today evolved from small dinosaurs who survived the mass extinction. They are the descendants of feathered meat eaters that walked on two legs and used their forelimbs as wings to fly, more than 150 million years ago. So dinosaurs are still with us, after all!

Take a look outside, and you might see a dinosaur!

Winners and losers

During the Cretaceous period, some groups of dinosaurs were extremely successful, such as plant-eating, beaked ceratopsians and duck-billed hadrosaurs. Other species declined, including stegosaurs and the long-necked sauropods.

Triceratops—a ceratopsian—was one of the last dinosaurs. It lived alongside T. rex.

Mass extinction

An asteroid 4.3 miles (7 km) wide crashed into the Earth near Chicxulub, Mexico. After the devastation of the initial impact, the dust thrown up made the world cold, dark, and inhospitable. The dinosaurs went extinct—or did they?

Dinosaur

Oryctodromeus was a small but special dinosaur that lived 95 million years ago in North America. These dinosaurs dug S-shaped burrows where they could hide from fearsome predators and withstand storms.

Going outside

The young dinosaur began to take trips outside the burrow to learn which plants were good to eat, and to strengthen its digging muscles. It stayed with its parents for several years.

Escaping the egg

A hatchling broke out of its egg using an "egg tooth" on its beak. This tooth was specifically for breaking the egg, and it soon dropped off. The babies stayed hidden, relying on their parents for food.

See also

Find out about other prehistoric creatures in "Dinosaurs through time" (96–97).

Laying eggs

Like all dinosaurs, Oryctodromeus laid eggs. It stored these safely underground in a den. The burrow entrance was narrow but opened into a larger chamber that was home to the nest.

Digging a burrow

When it was time to leave the nest, the young Oryctodromeus may have found its own territory and moved into abandoned burrows, repairing them. Alternatively, it could have dug its own burrow from scratch.

Mating

Males may have perfected their burrows—no female would want to raise chicks in a shoddy home! A female chose a mate and moved in to lay her eggs. Together, they built a nest.

Oryctodromeus fossils have been found in the burrows where they lived and died.

Puffin Today, some relatives of dinosaurs—birds—still live in dens and burrows. Puffin burrows are very similar in shape to the burrows made by Oryctodromeus.

Gopher tortoise These tortoises help out other wildlife. They make enormous burrows that provide homes for many different kinds of animals, including snakes, lizards, and rodents.

Safe from fire A burrow is usually safe during a forest fire because it's underground. The burrow retains moisture and the temperature stays low, even during a blaze.

Colorful crests

By the time the young pterosaur reached adulthood, its brightly colored crest was fully developed and may have been displayed to attract mates. Adults traveled long distances, searching for food and water.

Nest and eggs

Every year, the female Caiuajara returned to the same place to nest and lay her eggs. These eggs were soft-shelled and too delicate to be sat on—so the mother may have kept them warm under a mound of vegetation or buried them in sand.

As vegetation rots, it produces heat—this kept the eggs warm.

Fossil Pterosaur fossils show that their bones were hollow with thin walls, making them very light. This helped pterosaurs fly.

Oasis An oasis is created in the desert when water seeps up to the surface. This makes a fertile area for plants to grow and animals to drink and feed. Fossils found near oases tell us that Caiuajara lived near them.

*Caiuajara is thought to have been an **herbivore**—it ate only plants.*

Learning to fly

The chicks developed fast and were soon able to fly. They tested out their wing muscles by taking short flights while staying close to home.

See also
Find out about other prehistoric creatures in "Dinosaurs through time" (96–97).

Vulnerable chicks

The young were helpless at first and relied on their parents for food. The large group, or colony, provided safety in numbers for the fragile chicks.

Pterosaur

At the time of the dinosaurs, flying reptiles called pterosaurs dominated the skies. Caiuajara was a pterosaur from South America who lived around 91 million years ago, during a period called the Late Cretaceous.

Living together Today's colonial birds, such as flamingos, nest and breed in large groups. The discovery of a site containing many Caiuajara fossils, including eggs, babies, and adults, suggests that they lived in a similar way.

Sea turtle

Green sea turtles live in warm ocean waters and coastal areas. They spend many years swimming in the open ocean until they are ready to breed. Turtles come to the surface to breathe, and they lay their eggs on land. Female green sea turtles usually return to the beach where they were born to nest.

See also
Read about other sea animals, such as the lemon shark (88–89) and sockeye salmon (90–91), who swim to particular places to breed.

The female green sea turtle returns to land.

Returning home
About two weeks after breeding, the female leaves the water, usually at night. She climbs ashore to find a suitable place to dig her nest.

The mother lays eggs the size of ping-pong balls. Each nest of eggs is called a clutch.

Sea turtles can sense the direction of the waves, which helps them find their way in the water.

Laying eggs in the sand
After laying up to 200 eggs in her nest, the mother covers them with sand and returns to the water. She does this several times. The eggs are incubated (kept warm) for several weeks.

Breaking out
The temperature of the sand around the eggs determines whether the young will be male (cooler) or female (warmer). The baby turtle uses a special tooth to break out of its shell.

Warm seas
With flippers for limbs, sea turtles are perfectly adapted to ocean life. This green sea turtle is basking in the warm and shallow coastal waters of the Gulf of Mexico.

Protecting sea turtles
Sea turtles are endangered, and the survival of every baby is important. Turtle "head-start" programs give babies like this olive ridley a chance to grow up in captivity before being released back to the wild.

Mating in the shallows

The adults return to shallow waters, near their nesting beaches, to find food and to breed. Males will fight for a female by latching onto each other. Turtles often have several mates.

The lost years

Once in the ocean, the surviving hatchlings seem to disappear. No one knows exactly where they go. This period of time is known as "the lost years." The turtles take at least 25 years to mature before they start breeding.

Helpless babies

Baby sea turtles are very vulnerable to predators. Animals including land crabs, crocodiles, dogs, and sharks prey on the eggs and hatchlings.

To the ocean

Using their flippers as paddles, the baby turtles, called hatchlings, dig themselves out of the nest and scramble for the ocean. At night, the moonlight reflecting off the water helps them find their way.

Baby turtles are tiny—they are only about 2 in (5 cm) long.

Red-eared slider Like other freshwater turtles, the red-eared slider has clawed feet and a retractable head and limbs. The sea turtle has paddles instead of claws, and its body is streamlined for life in the ocean.

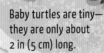

Sea kraits A type of snake, sea kraits spend most of their lives in the ocean but return to nesting sites on land to lay their eggs—just like sea turtles do.

Snake

The king cobra is the world's longest venomous snake. It can grow more than 16 ft (5 m) in length and preys mainly on other snakes. However, the king cobra has a caring side too. Many snakes abandon their eggs immediately after laying them, but the king cobra builds a nest for its eggs and guards them until they hatch.

Wrestling

In the breeding season, males fight over females. They raise their heads high and then wrestle, trying to pin their rivals to the ground. The defeated snakes slink away.

The king cobra raises its hood to make itself look larger than it really is and scare off predators.

Guarding the nest

The mother lies coiled on the nest, guarding her eggs. If she feels threatened, she opens her hood and gives a low hiss. She also raises part of her body off the ground. When really big king cobras rear up, they can be as tall as an adult human!

Babies hatching

Just before hatching time, the mother leaves the nest, leaving her babies to fend for themselves. In four to six years' time, the snakes will be old enough to breed.

The venom of the babies is as deadly as the venom of the adults.

Getting closer

When the winning male finds a female who's interested, he gently nudges her and moves over her. She spreads her hood in response, and they mate.

Making a nest

Looping her body, the female drags fallen leaves into a pile. She lays 20–50 eggs in the middle of the pile, then covers them with more leaves to keep them warm.

See also
Read how the female sea turtle (102–103) buries her eggs too—but doesn't stay to guard them.

Python shivers Most python mothers coil tightly around their eggs to protect them. Pythons living in cooler habitats also "shiver" their muscles to produce heat and keep the eggs warm.

Mom's fierce fangs A female rattlesnake gives birth to live young and stays with her babies for about a week or so. Any predator that comes too close risks a deadly bite from her venomous fangs.

Crocodile carrier Female Nile crocodiles help their eggs hatch by gently cracking them between their teeth. To keep the newborn crocs safe, they carry the babies to the water in their mouths.

Breeding colors

In spring, as the weather begins to get warmer, viviparous lizards come out from hibernation. The males molt, shedding their skin in flakes, and develop their brighter breeding colors.

Lizard

Most reptiles lay eggs, but a few lizards and some snakes give birth to fully formed babies. The viviparous lizard is unusual, in that it can do both. This lizard produces live young in places where it would be too cold for eggs laid outside to survive. In warmer climates, it sometimes lays eggs.

Love bites

During courtship, a male lizard grips a female with his jaws. If she accepts him, the pair mate. However, if she is not interested, she bites him fiercely and he backs off.

Carrying young

The female adjusts her body temperature so that it's just right for her young to develop inside her. She basks in the sun to warm up and hides in the shade to cool down.

Saltwater crocodile
The biggest reptile eggs are laid by the saltwater crocodile, which is the largest living reptile. Whether the baby crocs that hatch are male or female depends on the temperature inside the nest when the eggs are incubating.

Rubber boa
Bearing live young is more common in snakes than lizards. Roughly one-fifth of all snake species give birth rather than lay eggs. This includes the rubber boa, which can have up to eight babies at a time.

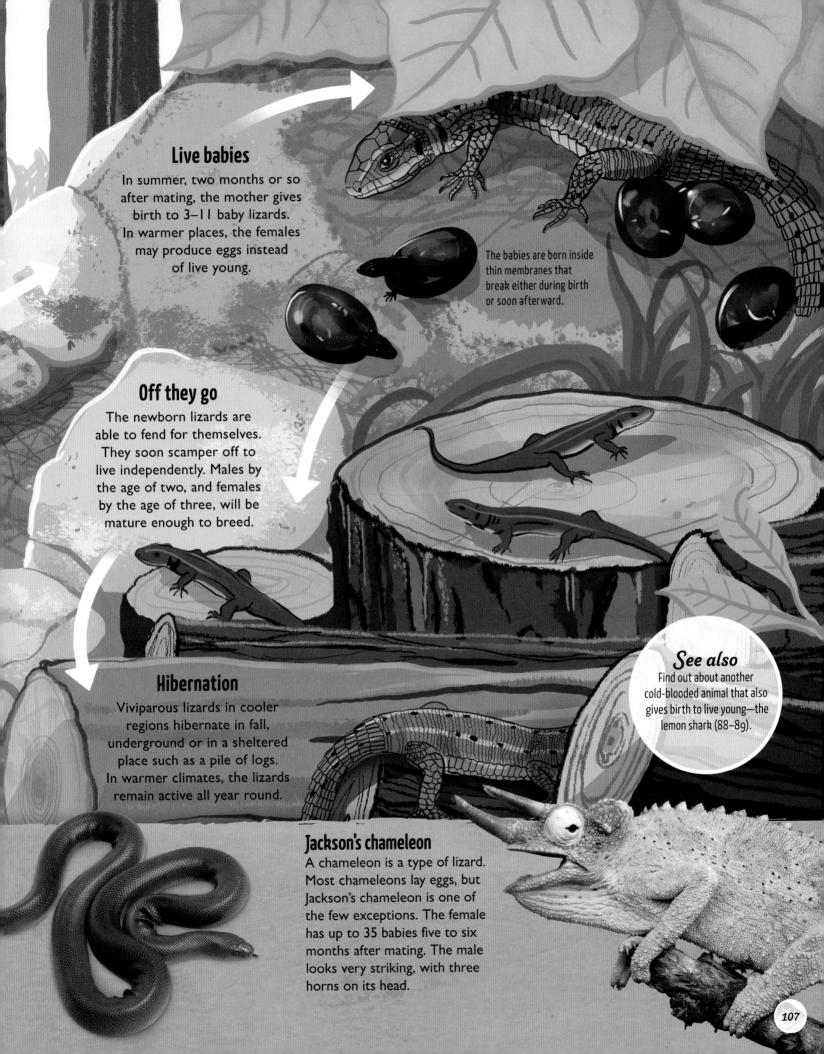

Live babies

In summer, two months or so after mating, the mother gives birth to 3–11 baby lizards. In warmer places, the females may produce eggs instead of live young.

The babies are born inside thin membranes that break either during birth or soon afterward.

Off they go

The newborn lizards are able to fend for themselves. They soon scamper off to live independently. Males by the age of two, and females by the age of three, will be mature enough to breed.

Hibernation

Viviparous lizards in cooler regions hibernate in fall, underground or in a sheltered place such as a pile of logs. In warmer climates, the lizards remain active all year round.

See also

Find out about another cold-blooded animal that also gives birth to live young—the lemon shark (88–89).

Jackson's chameleon

A chameleon is a type of lizard. Most chameleons lay eggs, but Jackson's chameleon is one of the few exceptions. The female has up to 35 babies five to six months after mating. The male looks very striking, with three horns on its head.

Penguin

Penguins are among the oddest birds that live on Earth.
For one thing, they cannot fly. Here, we follow the extraordinary
life cycle of emperor penguins in freezing Antarctica.

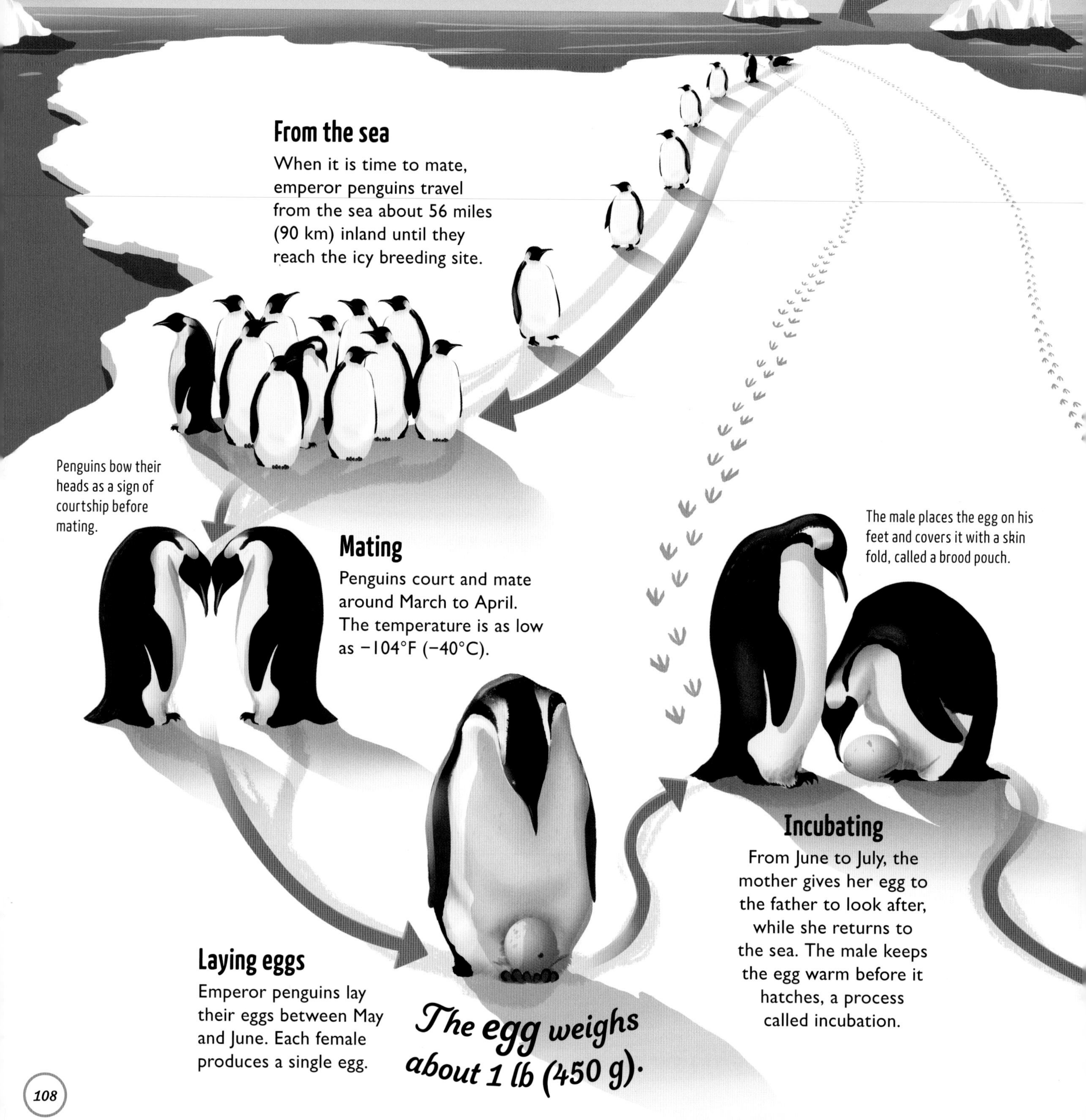

From the sea

When it is time to mate,
emperor penguins travel
from the sea about 56 miles
(90 km) inland until they
reach the icy breeding site.

Penguins bow their
heads as a sign of
courtship before
mating.

Mating

Penguins court and mate
around March to April.
The temperature is as low
as −104°F (−40°C).

The male places the egg on his
feet and covers it with a skin
fold, called a brood pouch.

Laying eggs

Emperor penguins lay
their eggs between May
and June. Each female
produces a single egg.

*The egg weighs
about 1 lb (450 g).*

Incubating

From June to July, the
mother gives her egg to
the father to look after,
while she returns to
the sea. The male keeps
the egg warm before it
hatches, a process
called incubation.

Return to the sea

Around January to February, the young penguin is ready to go to the sea for the first time. When it is about three years old, it will be ready to mate, and the life cycle can begin again.

See also
To find out more about life in extreme environments, see polar bears (124–125).

The parents take turns going to the sea to hunt, returning to feed their chick.

Molting

By December, the chick starts to molt—it sheds its down and starts to grow smooth waterproof feathers. This means the young penguin will soon be ready to swim.

By September, the chick can stand on the ice unsupported.

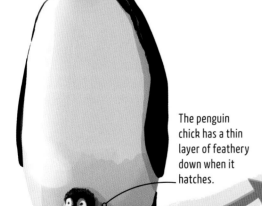

The penguin chick has a thin layer of feathery down when it hatches.

Feeding

The mother feeds her chick by bringing up food stored in her stomach. The food is like a paste or oil by this stage.

Hatching

The mother returns from the sea around August. Sometimes the egg has already hatched, but if not, she takes the egg back from the father. Once the egg hatches, she keeps the chick warm in her brood pouch.

Huddle
From October to November, while the parents are hunting for food, the penguin chicks huddle together in groups to keep warm.

Diving
Emperor penguins are great swimmers and divers. They can stay underwater for up to 20 minutes while hunting for food.

Enemies
Emperor penguins have few predators, but they have to watch out for leopard seals who might pounce and attack them.

See also
Find out about the orangutan (130–131), who also takes a long time to raise a small number of babies but can keep breeding for many years.

In their first year, wandering albatrosses are brown with white faces. They become whiter with age.

Leaving the nest
It takes around nine months for the chick to be old enough to fly and be independent. By this time, the parents are exhausted and will not breed again until the year after next.

Caring for their chick
The chick hatches with white downy feathers and grows quickly on a diet of fish and squid. Mother and father continue to share their parental duties—including fishing in the seas around the island.

Some albatrosses can still breed at 70 years of age.

Albatrosses have a good sense of smell, helping them track fishy meals.

Building a nest
Mother and father collect mud and grass to make a nest. They incubate their single egg for 78 days, taking turns sitting on the nest for two to three weeks at a time.

Albatross

Some animals breed slowly but live long enough to produce babies over many years. Wandering albatrosses manage this in a lifelong partnership. Males and females come together to produce just one egg every two years—but can remain as a couple for half a century.

Black-backed jackal A faithful breeding partnership works for black-backed jackals, just as it does for albatrosses—even their pups stick around to help their parents raise the next brood.

Albatrosses usually pluck food from just below the surface but sometimes plunge deeper.

Becoming a parent

It takes a long time for an albatross to grow up and become a parent. Couples won't pair up until both partners are at least 10 years old.

Prairie vole Most male voles mate with several females, but male prairie voles have a single partner and play an equal role in raising their babies.

Crested gibbon Daily grooming between the male (left) and female (right) helps strengthen the bond between gibbons, which is important for successfully raising their babies.

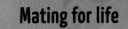

Mating for life

Albatrosses are alone for most of the year. But in November, they come together on remote grassy islands in the cold Southern Ocean, where they greet each other and mate.

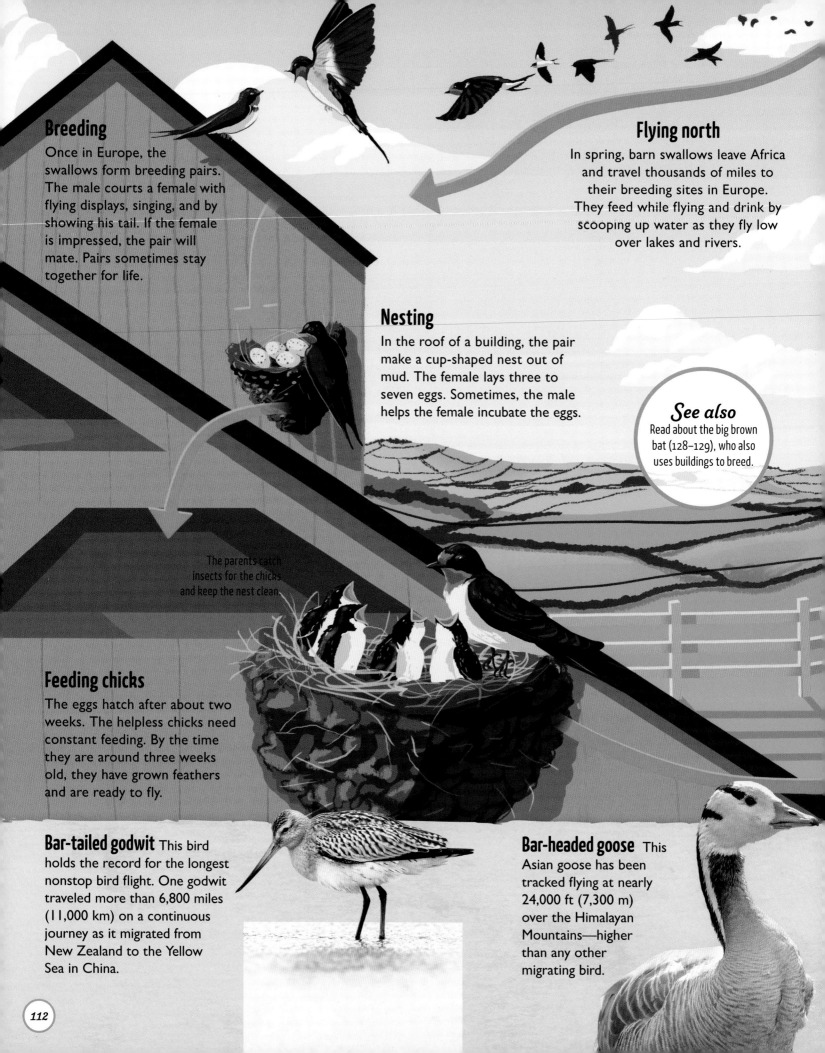

Breeding

Once in Europe, the swallows form breeding pairs. The male courts a female with flying displays, singing, and by showing his tail. If the female is impressed, the pair will mate. Pairs sometimes stay together for life.

Flying north

In spring, barn swallows leave Africa and travel thousands of miles to their breeding sites in Europe. They feed while flying and drink by scooping up water as they fly low over lakes and rivers.

Nesting

In the roof of a building, the pair make a cup-shaped nest out of mud. The female lays three to seven eggs. Sometimes, the male helps the female incubate the eggs.

See also

Read about the big brown bat (128–129), who also uses buildings to breed.

The parents catch insects for the chicks and keep the nest clean.

Feeding chicks

The eggs hatch after about two weeks. The helpless chicks need constant feeding. By the time they are around three weeks old, they have grown feathers and are ready to fly.

Bar-tailed godwit This bird holds the record for the longest nonstop bird flight. One godwit traveled more than 6,800 miles (11,000 km) on a continuous journey as it migrated from New Zealand to the Yellow Sea in China.

Bar-headed goose This Asian goose has been tracked flying at nearly 24,000 ft (7,300 m) over the Himalayan Mountains—higher than any other migrating bird.

Swallow

Often seen gliding over fields as they hunt for flying insects, barn swallows are swallows that breed among buildings. After raising their chicks, most that live in the Northern Hemisphere fly off to spend winter in warmer climates in the south. These barn swallows from northern Europe, for example, migrate to southern Africa.

Migration is tough: many birds die through exhaustion, starvation, or in violent storms.

Winter in Africa

When they reach southern Africa, the swallows' journey is over—for now. They spend the winter near wetland habitats, where the air is abuzz with flying insects to feast on.

Flying south

Barn swallows may raise two broods a year. In fall, after all their chicks have learned to fly, and after growing a new set of feathers, the swallows gather in large groups and fly south.

Arctic tern This record-holding bird makes the longest migration of all, from the Arctic to the Antarctic and back again—a total distance of 44,000 miles (70,000 km). It rests on the way, so it doesn't match the godwit for nonstop flight.

Starlings Migrating starlings often come together to form a huge cloud of birds that twists and turns in the air. Birds of prey find it harder to pick out individuals in the swirling mass.

113

Ready for inspection

When he is satisfied with his display, the male calls female birds to inspect his work. If a female likes the objects on show, she will mate with him.

If the male leaves his bower, even briefly, rival males may steal the most attractive pieces.

Simple nest

After mating, the female leaves and lays an egg in a simple nest that she builds in a tree. The mother raises her single chick alone.

The bowl-shaped nest is usually built 6–10 ft (1–3 m) above the ground.

Decorating the bower

On the lawn, the male bird places objects he has collected from the forest, such as flowers, leaves, berries, fruits, beetle wing cases, and feathers.

The bird arranges the objects into piles according to their color, size, and shape.

Care to dance? Grebes choose partners by dancing together on lakes and rivers. Great crested grebes present weeds to each other as they dance, while wiggling their feet rapidly to scoot across the water together.

Big red signal A male frigate bird chooses a nesting site and then inflates a bright red pouch under his throat to attract a female. He also shakes his outstretched wings and makes loud gobbling noises. All in all, he's hard to miss!

Building the bower

The male Vogelkop bowerbird weaves twigs and plant stems around a sapling (young tree). When the bower is finished, it looks like a little thatched hut with an arched entrance.

Bowerbird

For male bowerbirds, finding a mate involves a lot of hard work. They collect brightly colored objects and display their "treasures" beside structures, called bowers, that are made from twigs. Each bowerbird species builds a different kind of bower, and the Vogelkop bowerbird makes the most spectacular of all.

Bowerbirds are found only in Australia and New Guinea.

Creating a lawn

The bird clears the ground in front of the entrance to the bower. He then covers this area with a layer of moss, until it looks like a lawn.

See also

Find out how the emperor penguin (108–109) and the wandering albatross (110–111) form longer partnerships to look after their young.

Aerial displays To court a female, a male peregrine falcon performs spectacular stunts in the air. This is to show her that he is a skilled enough flyer to catch food for her, and for her chicks when they hatch.

Colorful character Striking colors and spiral tail feathers help a male Wilson's bird of paradise attract a mate. He calls to females and fans out his bright green chest feathers to impress potential mates.

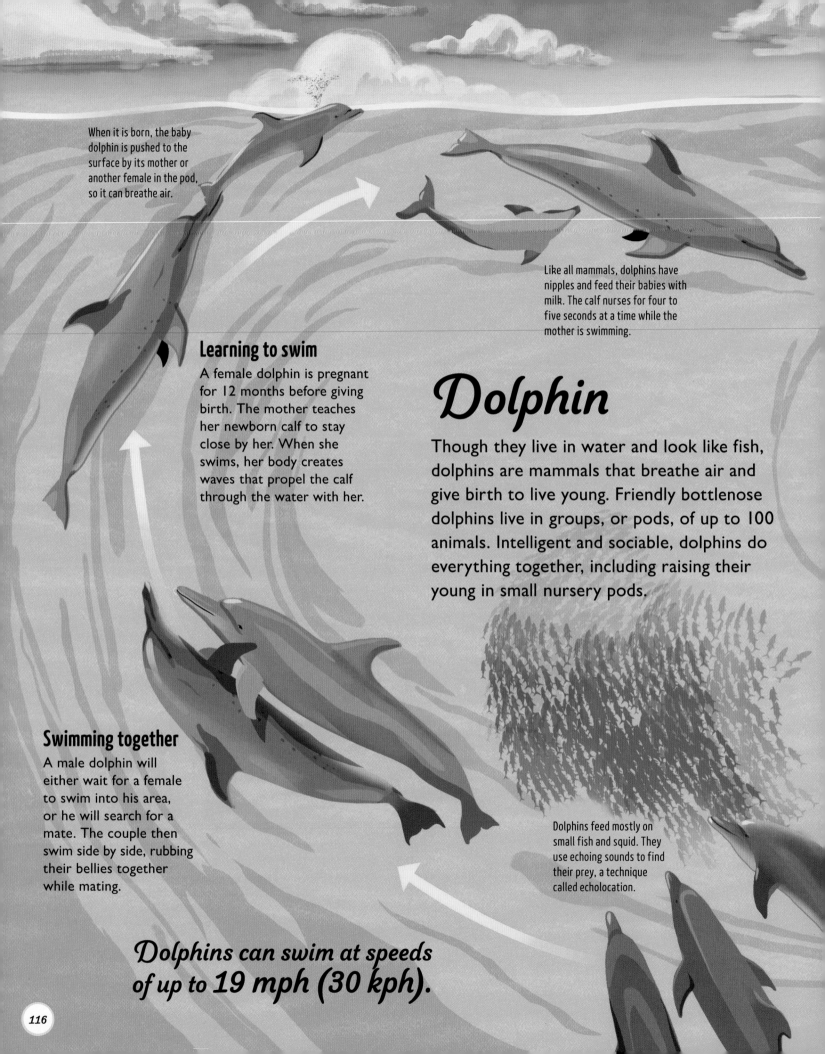

When it is born, the baby dolphin is pushed to the surface by its mother or another female in the pod, so it can breathe air.

Like all mammals, dolphins have nipples and feed their babies with milk. The calf nurses for four to five seconds at a time while the mother is swimming.

Learning to swim

A female dolphin is pregnant for 12 months before giving birth. The mother teaches her newborn calf to stay close by her. When she swims, her body creates waves that propel the calf through the water with her.

Dolphin

Though they live in water and look like fish, dolphins are mammals that breathe air and give birth to live young. Friendly bottlenose dolphins live in groups, or pods, of up to 100 animals. Intelligent and sociable, dolphins do everything together, including raising their young in small nursery pods.

Swimming together

A male dolphin will either wait for a female to swim into his area, or he will search for a mate. The couple then swim side by side, rubbing their bellies together while mating.

Dolphins feed mostly on small fish and squid. They use echoing sounds to find their prey, a technique called echolocation.

Dolphins can swim at speeds of up to 19 mph (30 kph).

See also
Read about lemon sharks (88–89), who also start their lives in the protection of a nursery.

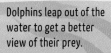

Dolphins leap out of the water to get a better view of their prey.

Females protect the calves in the nursery pod from predators such as sharks.

Nursery pod

Within each pod are small nursery pods, made up of mothers and their calves. Female dolphins even care for the calves of other females. This is called alloparenting.

Dolphin calves nurse for up to two years and stay with their mothers for three to six years.

Fully grown

Dolphins use sound to communicate with each other. Each dolphin has its own signature whistle. This allows them to recognize, find, and help each other.

Sperm whale Adult sperm whales dive deep into the ocean to feed. While some mothers go diving, others stay back to protect the calves in the nursery pod.

Horse and foal Just as a dolphin calf can swim as soon as it's born, so a horse's foal can stand and walk shortly after birth. They are both examples of precocious offspring.

Circle of defense Musk oxen protect their young from predators, such as wolves, by forming a circle. They stand with their heads and horns facing outward. The calves hide under their mothers in the center.

Kangaroo

Red kangaroos are the largest marsupials—mammals that carry their young in a pouch. They can be up to 6 ft (1.8 m) in height. Kangaroos use their strong legs and powerful tails to hop across the scrublands and deserts of Australia.

Females are usually smaller and grayer than the males.

Powerful male

The winning male may have fought off up to 10 competitors to win his chosen mate. He then checks if the female is ready for mating by smelling her urine (pee).

See also

Read about the sea horse (92–93), who also has a pouch—but it's the dad that carries the offspring, as eggs.

Carrying joey

After mating, the female is pregnant for only a month. The newborn joey is just 1 inch (2.5 cm) long—about the size of a lima bean. Shortly after birth, the joey climbs up into its mother's pouch.

The pouch protects the joey as it nurses and grows.

Suckling

The mother's pouch is lined with mammary glands that produce milk to feed her young. The joey finds a nipple and latches onto it—it can stay attached for up to 70 days.

118

Group life

Kangaroos live in social groups. Males compete for female partners by "boxing" with each other. They groom, kick, swat, and wrestle to find out who is the most powerful.

Kangaroos can reach top speeds of 44 mph (71 kph).

Joey pops out!

When the joey is strong enough, it starts to peek its head out of the pouch to look at the world. Even after the joey is too big to live in the pouch, it returns when it needs milk for several more months.

Wombat Unlike the kangaroo's, the wombat's pouch faces its rear. This means it doesn't fill with soil when the wombat is burrowing.

Opossum The female Virginia opossum gives birth to up to 21 babies, but she has only 13 nipples, so not all survive. However, she can nurse many babies at the same time!

Koala After growing in the pouch for seven months, a baby koala rides on its mother's back for several more.

Linked-up world

No living thing can manage on its own: all plants and animals rely on other life to survive. Each animal needs to find food—whether that is leaves, meat, or even dung. Each plant can grow properly only when nutrients from other organisms enrich the ground around its roots. Plants and animals are linked together in food chains that pass precious energy from one living thing to another.

Food web

The connections between living things are complicated. Many animals eat more than one kind of food. We call the links between the various plants and animals a food web.

Plants are green because they contain chlorophyll, which absorbs the sun's energy.

Many insects, such as locusts, feed on grass and other plants. They have mouthparts that can slice up vegetation.

Food chain

Plants take in the energy from sunlight and change it into food so that they grow. Herbivores (plant eaters) eat the plants, then carnivores (meat eaters) eat the herbivores. This series of connections is called a food chain.

Herbivores are called primary consumers because they are the first link in the food chain.

Plants are called producers because they produce food—they are at the start of the food chain.

Carnivores are called secondary consumers because they are the second link in the food chain.

Gazelles eat grass and other plants. They have grinding teeth for grazing and a stomach that can digest even the toughest leaves.

Lions pounce on gazelles and other animals and attack them with their powerful jaws. They use their sharp, stabbing teeth to cut through flesh.

Meerkats prey on locusts, scorpions, and other small creatures.

Scorpions eat locusts and other insects. They use their pincers to grab prey.

An eagle can swoop down and grab a meerkat in its sharp claws.

Cleaning up

In nature, nothing is wasted. Scavengers, such as vultures and hyenas, feed on dead animals. Decomposers, such as worms and dung beetles, break down plant and animal remains. This releases nutrients back into the soil and helps plants grow.

Vultures feed on the remains of dead animals.

Bacteria and worms break down material, such as the remains of dead animals after scavengers have taken their pick.

121

Stallions fighting

Zebras of the southern Serengeti mate and breed early in the year during the rainy season, when there is plenty of green grass to eat. Stallions fight each other over who will mate with a mare.

Stallions circle each other, bite, and kick out with their sharp hooves.

Nuzzling

Stallions and mares nuzzle each other before mating. The most important, or dominant, mare in the harem breeds the most often, and her foals rank higher than the others.

Zebra

On the open grassy plains of the Serengeti in eastern Africa, zebras live in family groups, called harems. A typical harem includes a stallion (male) and several mares (females) with foals. The harems gather in huge herds made up of hundreds, sometimes thousands, of zebras. Each year, the herds migrate. They are following the rains in search of fresh pastures.

Giving birth alone

Mares are pregnant for a little over a year. This means that the mares of the Serengeti have to travel long distances while pregnant. To give birth, the mother leaves the herd to hide from predators, such as cheetahs, lions, and hyenas.

Each zebra has a unique stripe pattern, like a bar code.

Moving on

Every year, herds of zebras join wildebeests to travel a clockwise circuit around the Serengeti, following the rains. By winter, they have returned south and are ready to give birth again.

Zebra foals

Most foals are born in January and February. The foals can stand soon after they're born, and they feed on their mother's milk for up to a year. The young are vulnerable to attack—predators kill about 50 percent of all zebra foals.

Oxpeckers like to hitch rides on the backs of zebras.

Cheetahs hide in the long grass and prey on zebra foals.

Oxpeckers These birds feed on parasites, including bloodsucking ticks, fleas, and biting flies, found on the skin of zebras. The bird's alarm call warns the zebra when a predator approaches.

Wildebeests Zebras and wildebeests are often found living in mixed herds, and both follow the Serengeti migration— though a wildebeest's pregnancy is shorter than a zebra's.

Giraffes Giraffes are also found in the Serengeti. However, because giraffes cannot swim or cross rivers, they do not follow the migration. They survive the dry season by nibbling on the branches of tall acacia trees.

See also
Find out about sharks (88–89), sea turtles (102–103), and emperor penguins (108–109), who also follow seasonal migrations to breed.

Hooded seal
Female hooded seals nurse for only about four days. Their milk has the highest fat content of any mammal, so pups grow rapidly and store fat (blubber) to keep warm.

Black rhino
The milk of the black rhino is one of the lowest in fat content of any mammal. Rhino calves grow slowly, nursing for as long as two years.

Pigeon
The pigeon is one of the few birds that produces a milklike liquid to feed its young. The liquid is made in a muscular pouch in the bird's throat.

Courtship
In early summer, bears that are mature enough—from around five to seven years old—start to mate. Males follow the scent trail left by female footprints. They are together for only a few days.

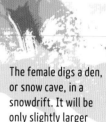

Preparing for birth
After mating, the fertilized egg doesn't start developing in the mother's womb until fall. This ensures that her cubs will be out and about in springtime, when there's more food. To prepare for birth, she digs—and then snuggles down in—a snowy den.

The female digs a den, or snow cave, in a snowdrift. It will be only slightly larger than her body.

Winter birth
Most female polar bears give birth to twins in December and feed them with fat-rich milk. The newborns are tiny, weighing about 1 pound (500 g). They are blind and covered with short fur.

The mother polar bear lives off her fat stores for up to eight months.

Growing up

Cubs grow fast on seal fat and will stay with their mom for two to three years. But when they become independent, they usually live alone and come together only to mate.

Hunting on the ice

Spring is a good time for hunting. Plenty of seal pups have been born, and there is lots of sea ice, so polar bears can get close to their prey. Hungry mom can regain her strength—and show her cubs how to hunt and swim.

Polar bear

Polar bears live and breed on the sea ice that floats in the Arctic Ocean. These fierce hunters are also strong swimmers and can stay in the freezing water for hours. Mother polar bears are protective of their cubs and will stay close by, watching over them as they play together on the ice.

By early spring, the cubs are ready to crawl out of the den.

Leaving the den

The mother's milk is very high in fat. It helps the cubs grow quickly. They stay snug in the den for a few weeks until they are strong enough to follow their mother to the edge of the ice.

See also

Read about the emperor penguin (108–109)—and how it gives birth during the polar winter too, but at the other end of the world.

*A polar bear's fur is see-through, and its **skin is black!** The bear looks white because it reflects light.*

Naked mole rat

No other mammal has a life cycle quite like that of the naked mole rat. These burrowing rodents live in large groups, or colonies, underground that are run kind of like bees in a beehive. One dominant female—the queen—produces all the babies.

Roots and tubers provide all the food and water that the colony needs.

One captive female produced more than 900 babies in just 11 years.

Powerful queen

The biggest, most aggressive member of the colony is the queen. Her presence alone is enough to stop other colony members from breeding. She can keep producing babies for 16 years—a long time for such a small rodent.

Workers moving into the queen's chamber huddle with babies to keep them warm.

Lots of babies

The queen produces bigger litters than almost any other kind of mammal. Every 12 to 19 weeks she gives birth to up to 28 babies.

A baby naked mole rat leaving the nest.

Moles

Mole rats are vegetarian rodents, while moles are worm-eating burrowers. They are fiercely territorial and live alone. Males and females come together only briefly to mate.

Meerkat families

Meerkats live in underground colonies, where a dominant pair produces the babies. Other colony members help with babysitting.

See also

Read about ants, who are also ruled by a dominant queen (78–79), and bats, another small mammal that lives in big groups (128–129).

The worker in front uses its teeth to dig, while others behind it kick the loose soil back.

Mature males

Unlike female workers, males stay fertile so they can father babies. When males wander into the burrows from other colonies, the queen selects her favorites and mates with them.

The most dominant naked mole rats are the ones who win shoving matches inside the tunnels.

Workers and soldiers

Babies grow up to become the workers of the colony. At first, they dig tunnels and collect food. As they get older, they become soldiers, defending the burrows from intruders.

New colonies form when tunnels get closed off and a new queen takes over on the other side.

Termites These sociable insects live in colonies dominated by a breeding queen and have workers to look after the nest or hive. Some termite species live in mounds, which have complex systems of tunnels.

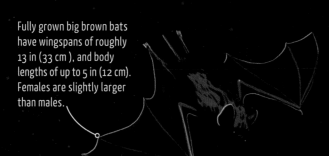

Fully grown big brown bats have wingspans of roughly 13 in (33 cm), and body lengths of up to 5 in (12 cm). Females are slightly larger than males.

Home to roost

By morning, bats have returned to their roosts—in tree hollows, caves, or buildings. As summer turns to fall and days get colder, bats fly less and spend more time in their roosts.

See also
Find out about polar bears (124–125), who also survive the winter by hibernating.

Summer hunting

The bats do most of their flying on warm, dry summer nights—when there are plenty of insects around. Some bats set out in the late afternoon, but most are active two or three hours after sunset. They will keep hunting through the night.

First flight

At three to four weeks old, the pups begin to take short flights. In order to catch flying insects in the dark, they learn a technique called echolocation. It helps bats find their way using sounds.

Vampire bat Vampire bats regurgitate (bring back up) blood they have digested from their prey to feed their pups. They even do this to feed bats from other families.

Echolocation Insect-eating bats use echolocation to find their food and avoid bumping into things at night. The bat calls out and then listens for an echo. If there is an insect or tree in the area, the echo lets the bat know where it is.

Mating and hibernating

Adults mate in September. During winter, when there are fewer insects around, the bats go into hibernation. Their body temperature drops, and they stop flying altogether. They lose weight but are able to survive on their body fat.

Bat

Bats are the only mammals that can fly like a bird. However, instead of feathers, they have wings made of thin webbed skin. Some bats eat fruit, but most munch on insects—this includes the big brown bat, found throughout North America.

Maternity

Although they mate in the fall, females don't actually become pregnant until after hibernation, in the spring. The pregnant females gather in maternity roosts. Their pregnancies last about 60 days.

*Bats are **helpful** to farmers—they **eat** insects that can harm crops and animals.*

Bat-sitting

From late April to early July, female bats give birth to one or two pups. Each baby bat is small enough to curl around your finger and is helpless for the first few weeks of its life. The females do all of the parenting, and they even babysit pups from other families.

Clever moth There is a particular species of moth that can interfere with the echolocation of bats. By disrupting the sound system, it saves itself from getting eaten!

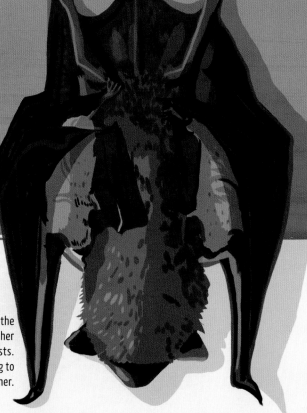

To save energy, the mother hangs from her feet when she roosts. The baby bats cling to their mother.

Orangutan

Orangutans are the largest tree-living great ape. They use their long arms and huge hands to move easily through the tropical forests of Indonesia. Their life cycle is slow compared to most other mammals. Mothers give birth once every six to eight years and have just four or five babies in their lifetime.

Mother and baby

Females are pregnant for around eight months. Once the baby is born, the mother bends tree branches to make a sleeping platform and builds a nest from leaves and sticks. The baby nurses for about two years and will stay with its mother for up to nine years.

Each night, the mother climbs up to her nest, with her baby clinging on tightly.

Pairing up

Orangutans pair up only briefly to mate. Females are attracted to the long calls of large, dominant males, which can be heard about half a mile (1 km) away.

Mature males have cheek pads called flanges—these are an added attraction to females.

Orangutans are more likely to breed when there is plenty of fruit growing on the trees.

See also
Find out about the wandering albatross (110–111), who also cares for its young over a long period.

130

Family life

Mothers keep their infants close by. Young orangutans make faces and signs to communicate. The mother teaches her infant how to find fruit and build a nest.

Orangutans eat mostly fruit and young leaves. They also feed on bark and insects, including ants and crickets.

Durian is the orangutan's favorite fruit.

Becoming adults

Young adults learn to climb trees and become skilled at using twigs as tools. Orangutans are not as sociable as other great apes. Generally they prefer to live alone.

California condor These birds will delay laying eggs so that they can take care of their existing young for longer—up to two years. Both parents help incubate the egg, feed the chick, and teach it how to fly. The chick stays in the nest for most of the first year. During the second year, the parents teach it how to hunt for food.

Elephant Like orangutans, female elephants take care of their young for a long time—up to eight years. At first, the babies stay very close to their mothers, learning how to keep up with the herd. Once they are a little older, the young elephants learn how to use their trunks and find food.

Humans *through* time

If you are reading this, you must be a human. Humans are the only species that has developed written language. It is one of many things we do that make us unique, along with speaking and making plans, for example. This is all thanks to millions of years of gradual changes, or evolution.

Stone hand axes were used for chopping and cutting.

Stone tools

Early humans began using their hands to make simple stone tools to chop up meat and plants. It was the beginning of the time period we call "the Stone Age."

Chimpanzees belong in our family tree.

Mammals evolve

The earliest mammals were small creatures that emerged from reptile ancestors. When a large meteorite hit the Earth, it ended the reign of the dinosaurs and left room for mammals to evolve.

Species split

Human and chimpanzee ancestors gradually began splitting into different species. While the ancestors of chimpanzees lived in trees and used their arms and legs to walk, our closest ancestors started to live on the ground.

By this time, our ancestors stood upright and walked using only their legs.

First in the family

At this time, there lived an animal who looked similar to the orangutans and chimpanzees of today. It is considered to be one of the first members of the family tree that includes humans.

Our ancestors began spending more time on the ground.

65
mya

3.5
mya

Our entire family is called the Hominidae, or great apes.

mya = million years ago
kya = thousand years ago

12
mya

10
mya

1.7 mya

100 kya

2.5 mya

12 kya

Eventually, people lived in all parts of the world except Antarctica.

Getting cleverer

Stone tools helped early humans eat a wider variety of food. The more skilled they became at making tools, the better they were at surviving. Toolmaking required thinking, so our smartest relatives became the most successful at staying alive.

Humans on the move

The first humans that were like us evolved in Africa. When some of them left, they gradually crossed into new continents. Some areas had cold climates and strange animals, such as the woolly mammoth.

Early settlers began farming crops and taming animals for milk and wool.

Hunting and language

As our relatives became more intelligent, they made tools to hunt large animals. It was dangerous work, so humans needed to plan and hunt as a team. This required clever thinking and a sharing of ideas, which led us to develop language.

Early people hunted woolly mammoths with spears.

Settling down

Humans had to move around regularly to hunt animals. Then some people began farming in one place. They built houses and farms, eventually forming towns and cities, trading with each other, and slowly building our modern world.

Infancy

During the first year, babies grow quickly but are completely dependent on their parents for care, food, and protection. As their muscles get stronger, infants start to crawl and eventually to walk. They may also speak their first words.

Childhood

Children grow steadily and learn skills, such as running, talking, and reading. They also learn to play with each other. All children develop at different paces.

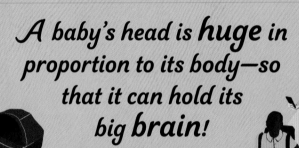

*A baby's head is **huge** in proportion to its body—so that it can hold its big **brain**!*

Giving birth

The mother's womb (uterus) contracts to push the baby into the outside world. Like all mammals, the baby is fed with milk. Mothers usually give birth to one baby at a time, sometimes two (twins), or occasionally even more!

Growing up

Teenagers, or adolescents, develop an adult shape and become more independent of their parents. They start to be able to sexually reproduce, in a stage known as puberty.

Fertilization

A man and a woman come together to make a baby. One of the female's egg cells joins with a male's sperm cell, in a process called fertilization. This is how all human life starts.

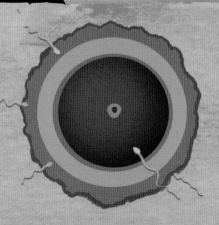

Embryo

Inside a female's uterus, the fertilized egg divides again and again to form an embryo, which is a tiny human made of millions of cells. At eight weeks old, the face, limbs, and internal organs are all in place.

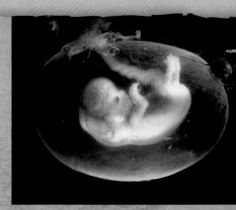

Young adults

By around the age of 20, the body is fully developed. Young people live independently and may form close sexual relationships. They may try to have children.

Middle age

Between the ages of 40 and 60, thinking and reasoning reaches a peak, although signs of ageing begin to appear. Some adults are still having children and caring for them. By later middle age, women can no longer have babies.

Old age

In this final phase of the human life cycle, clear signs of ageing appear. These can include gray hair, wrinkled skin, poorer vision and hearing, and stiffer joints. This "slowing down" can be lessened by regular exercise and a healthy diet.

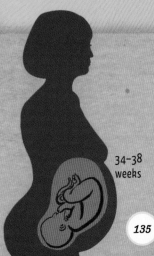

Humans

We are *Homo sapiens*—an intelligent species of mammal that can live for more than 100 years. Parents care for their young for many years, longer than most other mammals. Around the world, humans vary greatly—in terms of height, weight, appearance, and more.

See also
Read about orangutans (130–131)—a close relative of humans—who also look after their young for a long period of time.

Pregnancy The baby develops inside the mother for nine months until birth. At 12 weeks, it begins to grow nails. The baby can recognize its mother's voice at 24 weeks. A month later, the baby's hair starts to grow and the eyelids open.

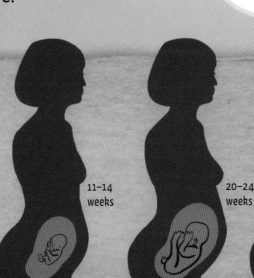

11–14 weeks

20–24 weeks

25–28 weeks

34–38 weeks

How *we* affect life *on* Earth

We humans have a devastating impact on Earth. We burn fossil fuels to power our homes and cities and create huge amounts of waste. We have been using Earth's resources as if they were unlimited and putting the lives of many species of animals and plants at risk. However, by changing our behavior, we can help protect the life cycles of other living things.

Problems . . .

Pollution

As the world's population increases, we are using up more resources and creating more waste. Cars, factories, and garbage pollute the air, land, and sea, harming animals and plants. Sea creatures eat plastic that ends up in the oceans, harming themselves and other animals that eat them.

Warming up

When we burn fossil fuels to produce energy, we increase carbon levels in the atmosphere. This results in global warming—hotter temperatures around the world, which have a dramatic effect on the environment.

Green energy

New technology allows us to generate energy without increasing global warming and pollution. Environmentally friendly— or "green"—energy sources include the wind, the waves, and the sun.

Destroying habitats

We use around 30 percent of all land for food, animal feed, and energy. The clearing of forests to create more land is called deforestation, and this has led to the loss of almost half of all trees. It also threatens the homes of many animal and plant species.

Wild farming

We can increase the variety of plants and animals in an area by growing diverse crops and restoring habitats for birds and pollinators—animals that fertilize plants. This practice is called wild farming.

Hunting

Hunters kill elephants for their ivory, tigers for their skin and bones, and rhinos for their horns. This practice, which kills millions of animals each year, is causing many species to die out, or go extinct.

Cutting down on waste

Recycling is the process of converting waste into new materials. Coupled with reusing objects instead of throwing them away, recycling helps preserve our resources and protect the environment.

*Species become **extinct** every day because of human activity.*

Glossary

abdomen part of an animal's body that contains digestive and reproductive organs

algae simple, plantlike living things that make their own food using energy from sunlight

alloparenting care given to a young animal by an adult that is not one of its parents

anadromous used to describe fish, such as salmon, that migrate from salt water to freshwater to spawn

asexual reproduction reproduction involving a single parent

atmosphere layer of gases that surrounds a planet

black dwarf dark, dead remains of a white dwarf star that has cooled

black hole region of space where gravity is so strong that not even light can escape from it. A black hole forms when a large star collapses into itself

breeding producing offspring (baby organisms) by mating

chrysalis pupa stage of a butterfly or moth

clone plant or animal that is a replica of its parent. Clones are produced by asexual reproduction

cocoon case made of silk that protects an insect while it is pupating

colony a number of living things of the same kind that live closely together

commensalism relationship where one species benefits, but the other neither benefits nor suffers harm

conservation working to protect the natural world

courtship animal behavior that forms a bond between a male and a female before mating

crust Earth's hard, outermost layer

deciduous plants that lose all their leaves at the same time, leaving the plant bare. They grow new leaves the following year

decomposing rotting or decaying. The bodies of animals and plants decompose after they die

drupe fleshy fruit usually containing a hard stonelike seed. Coconuts, plums, cherries, and peaches are drupes

egg fertilized female sex cell that develops into a new animal. Some eggs develop inside the mother's body, while others are laid. The eggs of birds and reptiles are enclosed by shells

egg cell female sex cell

embryo early stage of development of an animal or plant

endangered at risk of becoming extinct (dying out altogether)

erosion when rocks are worn down and carried away by wind, running water, or the moving ice of glaciers

evaporation when a liquid changes to a gas

evergreen plant that sheds and regrows its leaves all the time, so that the plant is never without leaves

exoskeleton hard, outer skeleton surrounding the body of some animals

fertilization fusing (joining) of male and female sex cells to produce a new living thing

fetus unborn mammal in the later stages of development

fruit ripened female part of a flower that contains seeds. Some fruits have a juicy wall to encourage animals to eat them and spread their seeds

fungi type of living thing that absorbs food from living or dead matter around it

galaxy very large group of stars and clouds of gas and dust

germinate when a seed starts to grow

hermaphrodite living thing that has both male and female reproductive parts. Earthworms are hermaphrodites

hibernation sleep-like state that helps animals survive through winter

host living thing that provides food for a parasite

igneous rock rock that forms when magma cools underground or when lava solidifies on the surface

incubate to keep eggs warm until they are ready to hatch

larva young animal that is quite unlike its parents and which changes into an adult by complete metamorphosis (plural: larvae)

lava hot, molten rock that erupts onto Earth's surface from volcanoes

litter a group of young born to an animal at a single time

magma hot, molten rock that lies under Earth's surface

mammary glands body parts of female mammals that make milk to feed their young

mantle Earth's soft interior, between its outer crust and inner core

mating coming together of a male and female animal during sexual reproduction

membrane thin barrier

metamorphic rock rock that forms when existing rocks are changed by heat and pressure to form new rocks

metamorphosis dramatic change in body shape as a young animal develops into an adult

migration seasonal journey by an animal to a new place, either to breed or to feed

molt how an animal sheds its outer skin regularly in order to grow

nebula giant cloud of gas and dust in space (plural: nebulae)

nectar sugary liquid produced by flowers to attract pollinating animals

nut hard, dry fruit containing a single seed

nutrient material taken in by a living thing to help it survive and grow

nymph young insect that looks similar to its parents but has no wings and cannot reproduce. Nymphs develop by incomplete metamorphosis

Pangaea supercontinent that existed about 320–200 million years ago, before breaking up

parasite living thing that lives on or inside the body of another species, called the host

parthenogenesis form of asexual reproduction in which offspring develop from unfertilized female sex cells. The young are clones of their parent

pod group of sea mammals, such as dolphins or whales

pollination transfer of pollen from the male part of a flower to the female part of a flower. Pollination is essential for sexual reproduction in flowers

polyp sea animal with a hollow cylindrical body and ring of tentacles around its mouth. A polyp is one of the life cycle stages of corals

predator animal that kills and eats other animals

prey animal that is killed and eaten by another animal

proboscis long, flexible snout or mouthpart. Butterflies and moths use a proboscis to suck nectar from flowers

protostar young star that forms when nuclear reactions occur in a hot, spinning clump of gas and dust

pupa resting stage in the life cycle of some insects, during which they develop from a larva to an adult through a complete change in body shape (metamorphosis)

red giant huge, bright, reddish star with a low surface temperature

reproduction production of offspring (young). Reproduction can be sexual or asexual

sediment tiny pieces of rock, the remains of living things, or chemical deposits that settle on the beds of lakes, rivers, and seas

sedimentary rock rock made from sediment. Layers of sediment get squashed and cemented together until they form rock

seed capsule containing a plant embryo and a food store

sex cell cell that is either male (sperm cell) or female (egg cell) involved in reproduction

sexual reproduction reproduction involving two parents

sperm male sex cell

spore single cell that Is produced by a fungus or plant that can grow into a new individual

supercontinent grouping of all or most of Earth's continents into a single, vast landmass

tadpole larva of a frog or toad. Tadpoles breathe through gills rather than lungs, and they have long tails

tectonic plate one of the pieces that make up Earth's rigid shell

territory area claimed by an animal, which it defends against rivals

umbilical cord long cord that carries blood between an unborn animal and its mother

uterus part of a female mammal's body in which a baby develops before it is born (also called a womb)

weathering when rocks and minerals are worn down into sediment

white dwarf dense, hot, glowing core left behind when a medium-sized star dies

Index

Acknowledgments

The publisher would like to thank the following for their kind permission to reproduce their photographs:

(Key: a-above; b-below/bottom; c-center; f-far; l-left; r-right; t-top)

11 Alamy Stock Photo: Granger Historical Picture Archive (cra). NASA: JPL / STScl Hubble Deep Field Team (cr). 12 Dorling Kindersley: NASA (bc). NASA: NASA Goddard (br). 16 NASA: Aubrey Gemignani (br); JPL / USGS (bc). 18 Getty Images: Chris Saulit (cla). NASA: ESA (bl). 22 Dorling Kindersley: Natural History Museum, London (bc). Dreamstime.com: Mikepratt (br). 23 Dorling Kindersley: Katy Williamson (bc). Dreamstime.com: Yekaixp (br). 25 123RF.com: welcomia (cra). 26 Dorling Kindersley: Dorset Dinosaur Museum (br); Royal Tyrrell Museum of Palaeontology, Alberta, Canada (bc). 27 123RF.com: Camilo Maranchón García (br). Dreamstime.com: Likrista82 (bc). 29 Dreamstime.com: Toniflap (cra). 30 Alamy Stock Photo: Nature Picture Library (br). Dreamstime.com: Kelpfish (bc). 31 Dorling Kindersley: Museo Archeologico Nazionale di Napoli (br). Dreamstime.com: Dariophotography (bc). 33 Alamy Stock Photo: Peter Eastland (cr). Dreamstime.com: Anizza (cra); Yurasova (br). 35 Dreamstime.com: Benjaminboeckle (cr); John Sirlin (cra). NASA: Jesse Allen, Earth Observatory, using data provided courtesy of the MODIS Rapid Response team (br). 37 Alamy Stock Photo: Tsado (br). iStockphoto.com: Francesco Ricca Iacomino (cra). 38 Dreamstime.com: Rudolf Ernst (bl). NASA: Jeremy Harbeck (bc). 39 Dreamstime.com: Staphy (br). 40 Dorling Kindersley: Oxford University Museum of Natural History (br). Dreamstime.com: Kseniya Ragozina (bc). 41 Dreamstime.com: Michal Balada (bc); Delstudio (br). 42 Alamy Stock Photo: Universal Images Group North America LLC / DeAgostini (cb). 43 Dreamstime.com: Digitalimagined (cl); Michael Valos (clb). 44 123RF.com: Pablo Hidalgo (clb). Dreamstime.com: Danakow (tr). 45 Dreamstime.com: Johncarnemolla (c). 46 Science Photo Library: Biozentrum, University Of Basel (bl); Dr. Richard Kessel & Dr. Gene Shih, Visuals Unlimited (cla); Steve Gschmeissner (cl). 50 Alamy Stock Photo: Krusty / Stockimo (ca). Dreamstime.com: Anest (cb); Hilmawan Nurhatmadi (clb); Martingraf (cr). 51 Alamy Stock Photo: Colin Harris / era-images (c). Dreamstime.com: Paulgrecaud (tr). 52 Dreamstime.com: Alima007 (br). Getty Images: Ashley Cooper (bc). 53 123RF.com: avtg (br). Dreamstime.com: Mykhailo Pavlenko (bc). 55 Dreamstime.com: Luca Luigi Chiaretti (crb); Hotshotsworldwide (cra). 57 Alamy Stock Photo: Stanislav Halcin (cra). 59 Alamy Stock Photo: imageBROKER (cr); Nathaniel Noir (cra). 60-61 Dreamstime.

com: Fiona Ayerst (bc). 61 Dreamstime.com: Ryszard Laskowski (bc). 62 Dreamstime.com: Max5128 (br); Photodynamx (bc). 63 Dreamstime.com: Jukka Palm (bl). 65 Dreamstime.com: Peerapun Jodking (cra). 66 Alamy Stock Photo: Rick & Nora Bowers (bl); Travelib Prime (cla). 71 123RF.com: Andrea Izzotti (cr). Dreamstime.com: Stephankerkhofs (cra). Getty Images: Auscape / Universal Images Group (br). 73 Alamy Stock Photo: F.Bettex - Mysterra.org (cr). Dreamstime.com: Jeremy Brown (br); Secondshot (cra). 74 Dorling Kindersley: Jerry Young (cl). Dreamstime.com: Benoit Daoust / Anoucketbenoit (bl). 76 Dreamstime.com: Rod Hill (tr). naturepl.com: Premaphotos (tc). 77 Alamy Stock Photo: Blickwinkel (tc). Dreamstime.com: Geza Farkas (tr). 79 Alamy Stock Photo: NaturePics (tr). 81 Dreamstime.com: Isabelle O'hara (cra). Getty Images: De Agostini Picture Library (br). 83 Alamy Stock Photo: Tom Stack (cra). Dreamstime.com: Isselee (br). 84 Alamy Stock Photo: National Geographic Image Collection (br). 85 Dorling Kindersley: Jerry Young (br). naturepl.com: Premaphotos (bc). 86 Dreamstime.com: Seadam (crb). naturepl.com: Alex Mustard (tr); Doug Perrine (cl). 87 naturepl.com: Uri Golman (tc); Norbert Wu (cl); Pascal Kobeh (cr). 88 Alamy Stock Photo: Image Source (br). 89 Alamy Stock Photo: Ross Armstrong (bc). Dreamstime.com: Nic9899 (br). 91 123RF.com: Michal Kadleček / majk76 (br). Alamy Stock Photo: imageBROKER (cr). 93 123RF.com: David Pincus (cr). Alamy Stock Photo: Helmut Corneli (cra); David Fleetham (br). 95 Alamy Stock Photo: Minden Pictures (br); Nature Photographers Ltd (cr). 99 Dreamstime.com: Altaoosthuizen (cra); William Wise (cr); Elantsev (br). 100 123RF.com: Iurii Buriak (br). 101 Getty Images: Frans Sellies (br). 102 Dreamstime.com: Asnidamarwani (br); Patryk Kosmider (bc). 105 Alamy Stock Photo: Avalon / Photoshot License (br). Dreamstime.com: Maria Dryfhout / 14ktgold (cr). 106 FLPA: Mike Parry (bc). 107 Dreamstime.com: Melanie Kowasic (br). 109 Getty Images: Fuse (cra); Eastcott and Yva Momatiuk / National Geographic (br); Paul Nicklen / National Geographic (cr). 111 Dreamstime.com: Isselee (cra). naturepl.com: Yva Momatiuk & John Eastcott (cr). 112 Dreamstime.com: Menno67 (bc); Wildlife World (br). 113 Alamy Stock Photo: Avalon / Photoshot License (bc). 114 Dreamstime.com: Mikelane45 (bc); Mogens Trolle / Mtrolle (br). 115 FLPA: Otto Plantema / Minden Pictures (br). 117 Alamy Stock Photo: Reinhard Dirscherl (cra). Dorling Kindersley: Jerry Young (cr). naturepl.com: Matthias Breiter (br). 119 123RF.com: Eric Isselee / isselee (br). Alamy Stock Photo: All Canada Photos (cr). Dreamstime.com: Marco Tomasini / Marco3t (cra). 120 Dreamstime.com: Tropper2000 (cra); Rudmer Zwerver (cr). 121 123RF.com: Andrea Marzorati (tl); Anek Suwannaphoom (ca). Dreamstime.com: Ecophoto (cl); Simon Fletcher (cr). iStockphoto.com: S. Greg Panosian (tr).

123 123RF.com: mhgallery (cr). Dreamstime.com: Chayaporn Suphavilai / Chaysuph (br); Mikelane45 (cra). 124 Alamy Stock Photo: Arco Images GmbH (cla). Dreamstime.com: Khunaspix (bl). 126 Corbis: image100 (bc). 127 Dreamstime.com: Volodymyr Byrdyak (br); Trichopcmu (bc). 128 Dorling Kindersley: Jerry Young (clb). 129 naturepl.com: John Abbott (bl). 131 123RF.com: Duncan Noakes (cr). Dreamstime.com: Rinus Baak / Rinusbaak (tr). 132 123RF.com: Uriadnikov Sergei (c). 134 Science Photo Library: Dr G. Moscoso (br). 136 Dreamstime.com: Smithore (cr); Alexey Sedov (cl). 137 123RF.com: gradts (cra); Teerayut Ninsiri (cr). Dreamstime.com: Cathywithers (clb); Elantsev (tl); Oksix (br).

All other images © Dorling Kindersley

DK would like to thank:
Caroline Hunt for proofreading; Helen Peters for the index; Sam Priddy for editorial input; Nidhi Mehra and Romi Chakraborty for hi-res assistance.

About the illustrator
Sam Falconer is an illustrator with a particular interest in science and deep time. He has illustrated content for publications including *National Geographic*, *Scientific American*, and *New Scientist*. This is his first children's book.